杨建文 著　　孙海琴 译

海的那一点点

杨建文诗集（汉英双语）

上海外语教育出版社
外教社　SHANGHAI FOREIGN LANGUAGE EDUCATION PRESS

图书在版编目（CIP）数据

　　海的那一点：杨建文诗集：汉文、英文 / 杨建文著；孙海琴译. -- 上海：上海外语教育出版社，2022
　　ISBN 978-7-5446-7370-9

　　Ⅰ.①海… Ⅱ.①杨… ②孙… Ⅲ.①诗集－中国－当代－汉、英 Ⅳ.①I227

　　中国版本图书馆CIP数据核字(2022)第174730号

出版发行：上海外语教育出版社
　　　　　　（上海外国语大学内） 邮编：200083
电　　话：021-65425300 (总机)
电子邮箱：bookinfo@sflep.com.cn
网　　址：http://www.sflep.com
责任编辑：王　璐

印　　刷：上海中华商务联合印刷有限公司
开　　本：710×1000　1/16　印张 10.75　字数 170 千字
版　　次：2022 年 10 月第 1 版　2022 年 10 月第 1 次印刷

书　　号：ISBN 978-7-5446-7370-9
定　　价：58.00 元

本版图书如有印装质量问题，可向本社调换
质量服务热线：4008-213-263　电子邮箱：editorial@sflep.com

序

初识建文先生，始于其书法造诣美誉，窃为他"独上高楼，望尽天涯路""衣带渐宽终不悔，为伊消得人憔悴"做学问的精神所感动。再识建文先生时，更惊叹于他还是一位诗人，一位中华文化艺术传播的使者，他的足迹遍及德国、法国、俄罗斯、秘鲁、日本、意大利、匈牙利等国，把中国书法艺术与诗词艺术传播到世界上爱好文化艺术的每一个角落，让世界人民感受中国传统文化的价值。今建文先生诗集英文版即将出版，邀我作序，我欣然提笔为本书作序。

善为诗者，不自命为诗人矣。其胸中所蓄，高广远矣。手握建文先生诗集手稿，沉甸甸，感其分量，悟其情怀。熔铸的人生质量，延展的人生境界，随着一页页翻开的墨水香气四溢弥散。那一个个熟悉的汉字，那一幅幅定格时代变迁的画面，恍然间若见诗人低头耳语，娓娓讲述着他对家国人生入乎其内、出乎其外的生气和高致。建文先生在诗中把对现实生活的关注、对人与自然和谐的发展、对人与人之间和睦相处以及对人类社会未来的信心交汇在一起，无论是"相知无远近，万里尚为邻"的高雅人生哲理，还是"各美其美，美人之美，美美与共，天下大同"的和处哲学，都以一种"润物细无声"的方式悄悄传递。

建文先生诗集全篇由十六个部分组成，前四部分描写了欧洲四国风土人情，后十二部分叙述了中国各地风土人情，中西对照，相得益彰。诗人用平实的语言描述了天道轮回，四季变换，人事更迭，家国情怀，字里行间充盈着对大自然的敬畏和对生命的哲思。青石板，鹅卵路，青峰丽水绿竹楼，这些西方所见又何尝不是东方文明的底色。人类只有一个地球，各国共处一个世界，我们一直在寻找人类共同利益和共同价值内涵的交集点，这些共同的底色又何尝不是呢？以艺术为底色，加强中外人文交流，促进中外人心相通，最终方能构建出超越文明冲突的人类命运共同体。建文先生诗集或许会给我们带来更多的遐思。

建文先生在诗意的阐发上丰富并幽深，用典深邃不露。"不著一字，尽得风流"，读建文先生的诗，需要更多的悟。"心地含诸种，普雨悉皆萌"。一景一情，一花一木，看似平淡，然细思量，此时此景此中意，已尽在纸上。很多学者用一个字归集中国文化根本之精神时，总是用到"悟"，细思还有什么字能更好地表达呢？唯"悟"不破！读一读建文先生的诗集，或许能领略到其中意味。

是为序。

陈燮君

Preface

I got to know about Mr. YANG Jianwen for the reputation of his calligraphy. I was moved by his academic spirit of assiduous and tireless pursuit of endless new height. When I met Mr. Yang again, I was even more amazed that he was also a poet and an envoy of the dissemination of Chinese culture and art. His footprints covered across Germany, France, Russia, Peru, Japan, Italy, Hungary and other countries, spreading Chinese calligraphy and poetry art to many parts of the world, facilitating peoples' understanding of the traditional culture. Today, it is my great pleasure and honor to be invited to write a preface to the English edition of Prof. Yang's poetry collection to be published soon.

Jianwen is good at composing poems but does not claim to be a poet. He has rich storage and wide coverage of knowledge. When I hold in my hand Jianwen's poem manuscripts, I feel the genuine weight and life inspiration. In the fragrance of the ink, I feel like touching upon the cast life quality and the expanded mind status. The familiar déjà vu of the handwritten characters, and the snapshots of the times, all are like the poet telling the stories or whispering the vitality and elegance of families, the nation and life. Prof. Yang makes it a convergence of his observation in his poems, of life observation, joint development of human and nature, harmonious coexistence of people, and a promising future for human society. He is spreading and conveying massages of life philosophy and arts of peaceful coexistence in a poetic manner. Sometimes, it is as philosophical as "Distance separates no bosom friends; thousands of miles apart we are still close neighbors". Sometimes, in reading his poems you may realize "Achieving one's own goal yields gratification; lending a hand to consummate others' goal doubles satisfaction; Goals of self and others can be unified; thus the world can be harmonized."

The collection consists of 16 parts. The first four parts describe the landscape and culture of four European countries, and the following twelve parts depict the scenery and local customs of many places in China. It presents us pictures of both the east and the west, and brings out the best in each other. In plain words, the writer is showcasing us about the laws of nature, turning of seasons, changing of people, love of family and nation. Between the lines is the writer's respect of the nature and thinking of life. The bluestone pavement, cobblestone lane, green hills, and the endless river across the city in Europe all have reflections and counterparts in China. They share a common bottom colour. Human beings share one unique earth. All countries coexist in the same world. We are searching for common interests and values of all mankind. Isn't the shared bottom colour one of them? Art serves as the bottom colour and foundation of cultural communication between the east and the west. It promotes mutual understanding and finally builds a shared future for mankind, beyond all boundaries and conflicts among civilizations. This is what the poem collection leads us to imagine and explore.

Mr. Yang's poetic interpretation is rich and profound, and the references and allusions are deep and implicit. "Without literal expression, you feel it romantic though". Reading Jianwen's poems requires insight and inspiration. "In the heart it fosters all seeds, and all sprout when it rains." Any scene, feeling, a flower or a tree, may seem insipid, but if you think and relate to the rich heart, they may already be a story. Many scholars use "Enlightenment" to illustrate the fundamental spirit of Chinese culture. Is there any better word though? I recommend you to read this collection of poems, think when you read, you may get inspired and enlightened.

By CHEN Xiejun

目　录

十一　康定秋韵

一　作客法兰西
A Visit to France

万里寻芳

（法国普罗旺斯观薰衣草）

恣意峰乱鸟林早，无情晚霞落棘巢。

孤傲自赏天涯客，万里寻踪一芳草。

注：今夏受邀赴德国弗莱堡大学讲学，闲暇之余，携夫人共往法国普罗旺斯一赏薰衣草之美景。七月正值赏花佳期，漫步于山田坡地，眼前犹如一块巨大调色板，各种色彩皆凝聚于紫色之中，显得那样祥瑞美丽，顿感诗兴大发。

Lavenders in July

The birds sing with the sunrise as they leave their nests in the
misty forest,
The lavender field is bathed in a golden hue as the sun sets.
With intense wanderlust and a passion for the beauty of flowers,
I travelled thousands of miles simply for a glimpse of the
beautiful lavenders.

Note: This summer I was invited to lecture at the University of Freiburg. My wife and I had the chance to go to Provence to admire the beauty of the lavenders there in July. We strolled about a sea of blossoms in which shades of all colors fused together into a vast purple plain. Enchanted by such beauty, I received the inspiration to write this poem.

小门洞天

（夜沉访雨果故居）

华灯孤影客愁新，不识昏墙步慢行。

莫言城僻巷尾深，小门洞天灿群星。

注：日落西窗初星风，华灯对影择时空。天南地北纵无限，人生如梦。步街黑灯形，无意街道景，向导遥指小门处，黑灯孤门话曾经。生时不由你，少壮须努力，两耳无须窗外事，无畏孤独长夜，无意惊天动地，只待群星耀地球，北斗东方启明。

Behind the Small Gate

Evening lights, a single shadow, my mind filled with sorrow.

Unfamiliar with the surroundings, my pace slows as daylight vanishes.

Never underestimate what lies behind a small and unassuming gate,

Behind its doors may lie a great shining star that can light up the sky.

Note: As the sun set and a breeze started to blow, the streetlights flickered, casting a lonely shadow on the ground. I felt myself transcending time and space. I have travelled all over the world, and still life is sometimes like a dream to me. The day gradually turned to night, though I had no interest in the nighttime scenery. My tour guide directed me to the small and unassuming gate of Hugo's former residence and shared many stories with me about the home. We cannot choose when we are born, but we can choose to make the most of our youth. Not distracted by irrelevancies, not afraid of suffering solitude in the long night, not intent on seeking fame, I just want to wait for the stars to shine on me, such as the Big Dipper and Venus.

牧羊女之歌

（大年初三梦醒奥尔良）

夜色随梦客仙家，雾苏贞嫒羞窗下。

烈火浴魂告天地，还醉江月牧羊茶。

注：异乡客梦，晨雾钟醒。好奇、等待、雾尽、惊艳，少女羞涩洁白的身躯，伟大而圣洁中透出端庄、平凡、豪迈而柔情。漫步街道，教堂钟声，转眼五百九十年（圣女）贞德涅槃太虚净。茶前饭后，牧羊女故事传吟。

Song of the Shepherdess

(A New Year in Orléans)

I dreamt in the depth of night in a foreign land,

Awakened to find a graceful shepherdess beside the window.

Her soaring aspirations beckon the world, she is not afraid to die,

I long to join her for tea as it brews under the mellow moonlight.

Note: I awoke to a thick mist and the sound of morning bells. Travelling abroad, I was curious in wonder when I noticed a graceful woman standing by a window. Her flawless beauty was pure, bold, and gentle. Strolling along the street amidst the chiming of church bells, I was taken back 590 years when the heroic deeds of the Shepherdess were on everyone's lips.

西城东梅

（市政大厅书法展感怀）

春早西城风犹寒，东池二月梅初放。

无怨墙根孤残雪，香盈政殿满庭廊。

注：东方晓，西方明，新桃旧符唤春临。大年盈喜气，应邀法兰西。异域景，风土情，艺术之都人文兴，市政大厅通火亮，展新作，举杯东方韵。

Plum Blossoms

In the chill early spring wind, outside Hôtel de Ville

Plum blossoms are all blooming.

With snow remaining in the corner of the wall,

Their fragrance overflows the corridor and hall.

Note: At the best time of the year, when the Chinese Spring Festival falls and everyone back home is busy putting up peach wood charms, I am invited to the French city of Orléans, to host my own calligraphy exhibition. Though thousand miles away from each other, I feel that both peoples, French and Chinese, share the same passion for beauty. Alas! What an honor it is, to present, here in a city of art and culture, my newly completed pieces, to share with my French friends, the essence of oriental art as a humble old man understands.

痴潮

（昂布瓦兹瞻仰达芬奇故居）

朔风疏桐日冬篱，大路无声布天底。
村头小屋纳四海，痴潮如斯呼芬奇。

注：文艺复兴，三杰分庭，百年无声各远去，带不走功业曾经。地球东西，人类物器，盛名一世生有限，无为乐乐充光阴。望日光偏西，室空寒气，四海无约聚一隅，无语心路追记。

A Visit to Leonardo da Vinci's Residence in Amboise

On a cold winter day we come to the town of Amboise, where
The brutal winter wind is battering the sycamores, and
A wide road stretches into the distance against the cloudy sky.
Soon we come to our destination at the north corner of the town, and see
A crowded small chapel — how come it is favored by so many visitors?
This is where the great master Leonardo da Vinci rests in peace.

Note: The visit to Leonardo da Vinci's former home reminds me of what I learnt about the Renaissance, when masters like him, Michelangelo and Raffaello created some of the most well-known pieces in the history of art. Now they are long gone, but their best pieces remain among the most precious treasures of mankind. Like all of these masters, everyone on earth lives a limited life. No matter how much fame we gain, it merely matters when we leave this world — isn't it true that life is just a passing dream? But let us not be too sad. After all, we still have this moment, here in this small chapel, with visitors coming from across continents and oceans, sharing the same love for art — and that makes the trip worth it.

童薪红炉

（奥尔良郊王丹家中做客）

野旷林穷曲折路，一隅红墙抵寒暑。
窗外千树争鸟鸣，独善童薪旺火炉。

注：天苍苍，路何处，愁煞人穷无助。近尺咫，自眼下，小人寸鼠目。抬望眼，望不及，天涯无尽遥无计，举足君子步。地茫茫，家安路东西。床自南北头，无泥不屋人千里，纵缘婵娟听诉。旧友相聚，转眼春秋十年，十年光阴织短长，各自勤家业。家兴酬勤人，人疏地生更辛苦。喜望童稚，薪火加添，温暖寒舍爱无数。

Fresh Wood in a Sizzling Fireplace

(A Visit to Wang Dan's Home in Suburban Orléans)

At the bottom of a road winding across an open field,
Stood a red-brick cottage sheltering people from heat or chill.
Outside the window are the birds amid forests happily chirping,
Inside the cottage is the fresh wood fed into the fireplace
sizzling.

Note: In my life pursuit I often feel sad and helpless, for the road of life seems boundless, yet I do not know where it leads. Looking backward, I've seen short-sighted villains who come close to me with their tricks and traps. Looking forward, I know not where the road turns towards, but only hold my virtue tight. The world is big and people settle down east and west, hoping ups and downs in life will all go through. Despite all the twists and turns, luckily, friendship always brings them together from miles afar. Oh, my old friend, it has been a decade since we last met. How time flies now we have both devoted to family life for years! It must take hard work to live here on this foreign land, but isn't it gratifying to see all your effort paid off? Watching your grandson feeding wood into the fireplace, I feel warm and delightful, for he is filling love to this house.

流金双影

（ 王丹家后院林间小道漫步 ）

十年缘出一日新，酒饱犹兴云乡径。
无意落日孤林后，流金叶地对双影。

注：缘何解，无人知，世上多巧事，无巧不书。分合离散说人世，天涯无计路途。老友重逢说新朋，举杯情洒篱屋。酒后多珍言，光阴不停步，不觉晚风绕西窗，红日徘徊林渚。密林深处是我家，碧草参天树，林深径直望不尽，只留孤轮倩影，双双鸿雁归路。

Two Golden Shadows

(A Ramble on the Shady Path in Wang Dan's Backyard)

Our friendship never grows old though ten years have passed.
After wined we still enjoyed a ramble in your backyard.
The sun sank unwittingly into the lonely forest,
Casting two golden shadows on the leaf-strewn ground abreast.

Note: What is the so-called "fate"? Why has it brought up so many coincidences? No one has a clear answer, and that's why people have written numerous stories. Here in your little cottage we gather — isn't it delightful to meet friends from afar? Here we share our sorrow and joy, talking about new friends and giving a genuine toast to our friendship. Merrily we drink and talk, as if we had forgotten how time had passed by. The night wind is hovering around the window, while the sun is sinking slowly behind the forest. Where this cottage lies deep into the woods, is a place encompassed by green grass and towering trees. Down from the door lies a shady path, stretching into the distance. Looking above into the sky, I see the sun still lingering, and we, like a pair of wild geese, are heading back side by side.

泥板忆古

（奥尔良做客伊朗书法家）

草园深巷半篱门，寒壁勤薪尚衣冷。

断苇湿泥聊古事，含毫五德开泰魂。

注：西域说文明，东亚古国邻，中国、印度、巴比伦，文字诉国情。文字起象形，幼发拉底波斯兴，湿泥断苇楔形字，汉谟拉比典法令。古国不再时，古字早退尽，天下字母二十六，唯看汉字强生命。真、行、篆、草、隶，书法步古今，众家追求精气神，书艺无止境。今日得机缘，作客异国论书艺。他笔字游戏，吾作水墨形。互倾异国字，筑美人文情。

Remembering Things Past

(A Visit to an Iranian Calligrapher in Orléans)

In the garden tucked in the lane with its fence half closed,

The burning fire and the clothes on my back could not

withstand the bitter cold.

Among the withered reed and wet mud, we reminisced about

things past,

Fully indulged in wielding the writing brush, consoling our

longing hearts.

Note: Long embedded in the history, ancient China, India and Babylon in Eastern Asia were not far from each other. We talked about the ancient civilizations of China, India, and Babylon and their ancient characters which originated from pictographs and flourished along the Euphrates in Persia. Later, when the Hammurabi Code was in place, cuneiform became popular. Chinese characters live on whereas other ancient forms of writing have been replaced by twenty-six letters. Represented by regular script, running script (semi-cursive script), seal script, cursive script, and clerical script, calligraphy has been passed down throughout history. The pursuit of calligraphy has always been the inner spirit. The journey of refining the art of calligraphy knows no end. This opportunity allowed me to discuss calligraphy in a foreign land. My friend wrote as I accompanied with Chinese ink painting. Such a wonderful display of cross-cultural beauty.

旧宫怨

（游香波尔城堡有感）

晨风马蹄踏宫门，古堡群楼钟鼓沉。

环步琼阶前朝曲，直眼空室寒鸦声。

注：天下苍生妈妈宠，人凡各殊命不同，何不同，隔门洞，宫室琼楼望不及，佳丽万千情何从。声声呼上苍，权力由谁供，世多难言事，无论东西南北中。

A Visit to Château de Chambord

In the morning breeze I came to the beautiful Castle of
Chambord, where

The towers stood majestically and the bell was tolling in a low
sound.

Walking around, I started to imagine about the life of its former
owners, when

Suddenly, my thoughts were interrupted by the call of jackdaw
up on the roof.

Note: Though most of us are cherished and taken care of by our parents when we are
young, not everyone could manage to live a happy life from birth to death. Walking in
the Castle of Chambord, I am quite convinced that every and each owner of this palace
has led a luxurious life. But does this mean their happiness was ensured? No, and not
to mention hundreds of thousands of those from ordinary families. Yet I cannot help
wondering why men are born so different — some born rich, some born poor; some
born with supreme power, while some even deprived of basic rights. Who is the ruler of
all this? Perhaps only the wind knows.

锦桥点春

（游法国花园小镇科尔马）

天工无意晚风微，朝露悉心宛城翠。

繁花问得谁为巧，锦桥羞鞚点春归。

注：初灯夕霞寻路，街空人静地疏。隐隐远处展酒旗，夜黑还梦庐。天边晨风吹起，难忘昨夜意未了，复寻小城司仪。穿穷林，过街道，钟声传世纪。小城童话里，街窗水草吐露珠，桥头古堡，鲜花奇葩，望不断香如故。马蹄朗日乱花舞。人生纵有千般乐，尽情岁月殊。

Saint-Pierre Bridge in Spring

Last night I roamed streets engulfed in the carefree breeze,

This morning I found the town dressed in green and covered in dew.

Flower blossoms ask in wonder who will help them flourish,

The bridge responds that spring is returning to nourish.

Note: The sun was setting and the streetlights were on as I strolled down the tranquil streets of Colmar. The streets were empty but a flag fluttering indistinctly in the distance. After nightfall, I returned to the hotel and fell asleep. The next morning, my heart was still longing to explore. My tour guide and I explored the forest and walked through the streets as the sound of bells rang. In the fairytale town, dew covered the plants and the bridge led to a magnificent castle. The vast expanse of fragrant flowers danced with the wind as men and women lived a joyous life to the fullest.

今故史步
（法国中世纪小城福卡尔基耶）

山笼晚风钟古巷，巷空石台谙绯窗。
窗隔楼柱静九门，霞瑟余音袅史廊。

注：星月交错，辰霞重复。漫步山城赏光景，不觉时光倒数。任意随风街道，静现老墙旧屋，风雨飘摇数百年，无思新处。抹不去，民族魂率世代情，岁岁雄鸡唱高卢。有心寻梅柳，无意遇旧故，山城风光藏深巷，顺楼环步。今夜月正好，深闺传琴瑟。满心异域探新异，此处尽好古。

A Stroll Transcending Time

In the evening, the mountain breeze often favors the old alleys.
Dark red windows and stone steps decorate the narrow paths.
Ancient arches accompany the windows and columns,
The stringed melody echoes off of the arches under the evening glow.

Note: The morning glow can't wait to emerge while the moon still hangs in the starry sky. Wandering the town while searching for its beauty, time passes in an instant. Being directed by the breeze, I suddenly came across beautiful medieval houses. These walls have survived centuries of wind and rain. The spirit of generations also lives on in these ancient structures and has been represented by the Gallic rooster since the Middle Ages. I set out on a sightseeing journey but ended up experiencing the cultural legacy of the area. To unlock the hidden beauty in this town, one must explore the local residences along the winding paths. The moon was beautiful and it was wondrously complemented by the harmonious music coming from one resident's boudoir. I travel in search of new and exotic places, and the town of Forcalquier is an ideal destination which is steeped in historic charm.

二　德国风

Townscape in Germany

泛舟莱茵河（一）

晨光津渡静他乡，青峰丽水两漫漫。
四海船客八方走，波开舷头别梦寒。

注：初游莱茵河，体味他国豪艇坐，绿水青山无两样，田园齐正如诗如画美农舍。

Cruising the Rhine I

The boat departs with the rising sun

Which casts a glow on the tranquil foreign land.

Endlessly the river flows amid green hills.

The stream comes from afar and flows into new lands,

Not unlike the passengers longing for an adventure.

The bow breaks the waves ferrying them on their journey.

Note: My first trip down the Rhine reminds me of the natural beauty of my home. The beauty of the green hills, the flowing river, the fields, the trees, and the countryside is poetic and picturesque.

泛舟莱茵河（二）

寒水知寒思新浪，浅底鱼翔竞白帆。

回首古堡斜雨后，风动钟琴更华章。

注：今作闲散客，思绪万千心头河，继往开来钟声远，山势随波，一路静观古堡多。

Cruising the Rhine II

The cold depths of the Rhine crave for new waters.

The fish roam up and down along the shallows,

Racing the boats which float overhead and under the sky.

In the distance an ancient castle stands strong in the rain,

Where the carillon sound has gone with the wind.

Note: Cruising the Rhine as a myriad of thoughts run through my mind. Behold, the ancient castles standing solemnly on the hills along the winding river. The ringing bells of the clocktower are perhaps remnants of the same travelling through time.

过黑森林

风行八百过山蹊，层林竞墨无穷碧。

树高千丈叹黄叶，入土化魂复芳菲。

注：德国有片黑森林，不知黑树是何形，赤橙黄绿青蓝紫，自然常态叶分明，何言黑森林。今晨驱车入其境，见山势连绵，古木参天，遮云蔽日数百里。因其森林覆盖，故而为曰，黑森林也。

Through the Black Forest

Hundreds of miles across mountains and rivers
Takes me to a vast expanse of infinite shades of green.
Mighty trees, please don't sigh for your fallen leaves,
For they begin a new journey from the ground.

Note: I was always curious about what the trees looked like in the Black Forest. Were they different from normal trees? Did they grow in different shades of green than other trees? One morning, I decided to go and see for myself. I found myself gazing upon rolling hills and lofty trees extending hundreds of kilometers. I realized that the Black Forest got its name due to how marvelously thick the woods are.

雨市弗莱堡

日暮林空客他乡，一宿风雨行路忙。

流云可知客人心，灯火阑处说惆怅。

注：晨风滴滴湖，晚霞弗莱堡，赏不尽琼楼异域景。古堡钟阙横街心，车水马龙穿堂室，正好奇，不防飘雨碧天倾。湿身方寸动，衣冠乱心情，在家千日好，出门半时难，游子万里无牵挂，剪不断，孤灯窗下慈母影。

Freiburg in the Rain

Sunset in an empty wood,

At the foreign land I arrive,

After a hurrying night,

All cloudy and rainy.

O, drifting clouds, can you tell

A stranger's heart in the dim light,

When melancholy holds it tight.

Note: Titisee lake in morning breeze, Freiburg in sunset, these were the exotic yet magnificent scenes my eyes feasted on. My curiosity was aroused by an old bell tower standing in the middle of the street with traffic going through it, but a sudden sun shower interrupted. Wet and in a mess, my mood grew increasingly sour. "East, west, home's best." I thought to myself. Men, however far away from home, will always miss but one thing: their loving mother back home, who'd lean against the window while sinking into thoughts of her boy.

华夏之夜

（弗莱堡大学孔子学院畅书）

红灯绿竹西楼诗，星月流空东篱词。

泱泱和声裹丝弦，有识天涯共此时。

注：四季长轮回，光阴无反顾，夜观月亏月盈时，心往何处。身在异乡万千思，今夜星光楚楚。西楼高红灯，丝弦和琴素，绿竹睡园花解梦，群贤席坐依次。初识安娜也有幸，外冷淡，内柔情，纯洁坦然，尽显民族风韵。时光匆匆叹不及，孤灯夜散人影。

Beautifully Homesick

Up in the west tower, we write poems among the green bamboo
and red glow.
Down beside the east fence, we compose Ci under the starlit
sky and bright moonlight.
Melodious chords flow from the stringed instruments,
We are reminded of home, and are hearts fill with
homesickness.

Note: While the four seasons are constantly coming and going, lost time never returns. One starry night, I met with a group of teachers who teach at the Confucius Institute of the University of Freiburg. Homesickness filled our hearts as we appreciated the moon's glory. The lights high in the west tower emitted a warm red glow. The gathering, beautifully accompanied by traditional Chinese string instruments, could be compared to the banquets hosted by the Prince of Xiao of the Liang State. It was there that I became acquainted with Anna. Behind her unassuming appearance I discovered great tenderness and purity. The evening's moments flew past and suddenly the room was empty. Only the red glow remained.

大地魂

（观德国科隆大教堂有感）

洪荒苍茫大地魂，振壁蜉蝣六百春。
无是夜郎枉自大，一举临云擎天门。

注：中国庙宇，欧洲教堂，人类文明，艺术华章。科隆之地尽灵气，叹杰作，前仆后继六百年，尽显人类力量，民族功底。天地同存，地球共生，五洲光阴皆一体。四海芳草有差异。你说快，我说慢，时下有奇迹。三周完成万丈楼，问天地，快慢全凭你自己。

Soul of the Land

(A Visit to the Cologne Cathedral)

O'er six-hundred years the soul of this ancient land was built,
It now towers above its surroundings.
Humble is the Cathedral about its height,
As its steeples reach towards the mighty sky.

Note: Ancient temples and churches represent cultural and artistic legacy. The Cologne Cathedral, a masterpiece completed over a six-hundred year period, characterizes human capability and national pride. We as humans are all unified by one world and one time. That being said, we are all different and on occasion can create masterpieces. A Cathedral over six-hundred years or a skyscraper in three weeks, which do you prefer?

镇子

（晨步德国小镇吕德斯海姆）

晓语金路小山城，翠岗紫葡列辕门。
醇逸随风藏深巷，未杯先醉感酒魂。

注：吕德斯海姆，德国一小镇耳，以美酒闻名。今夏携夫人游于此，晨风里，悠悠漫步。一路酒肆招彩旗，山背葡井珠满坡，红霞犹兴夜未尽，巷深肆浓醉客多。

The Town

(A Morning Stroll in Rüdesheim)

Strolling down a countryside road showered by golden rays,
In the vineyard painted purple with hanging grapes.
I am intoxicated by the fragrance of a full-bodied wine
Carried over me by the gentle breeze.

Note: One summer morning, I visited Rüdesheim with my wife. As we walked around in the small German town acclaimed for its fine wines, I was impressed by the number of bars which lined the streets. The nearby valley was lush with purple grapes and people enjoyed the bars and the wine they served from sun down to sun up.

夜宿菲森乡村小酒店

绿树连排芳草地，长空无尘透心碧。

黄花尽头日落处，天边纵霞隐酒旗。

注：农村与城市，何以好坏分。车水马龙，高楼林立，一派商铺街景。灯红酒绿说君子，霓尚时潮人。桃花纤云，麦浪无边，点点篱院落仙境。自然生态天人和，美哉农村。

Stopping Overnight in a Füssen Village Inn

Green trees line the grassed land,

Below a cool azure sky free of dust.

Beyond yellow flowers the sun sinks,

Afterglow on the horizon hiding pub signs.

Note: Village or city, no one is to say which is better. A city means flowing traffics, skyscrapers, and streets crowded with shops, where night was bustling with bright lights and so-called fashions. A village, though, means untainted beauty of nature — peach blossoms below light clouds and waves of wheats dotted with fenced yards — where heaven and humanity meets.

三　瑞士小憩

An Episode in Switzerland

水榭问

（瑞士卢塞恩登阿尔卑斯山）

小城欲晓出辕门，晨风吹散玉波纷。

心帆圣渺湖山过，定眼尘埃略仙魂。

注：天地异功，人类福同。山仁水智乐生命，生者切亡从。有人喜雕宫，也有逸野风，无知生命乐何处，举步途穷。滴水须思源，水活天人共，一砖一木愿天地，生成亿万功。静听平湖碧波，绿稼鸥鹭鸣凰，羽轮翱空舞彩云，年复一年，生生不息梦。瑞士美湖光，山色益葱荣，沿湖处处雕宫落，泥木水尊重。尽显人间知双手，并非上帝宠。漫步湖堤杯释酒，感受人文风。

Pondering at the Waterside Pavilion
(A Stay in Lucerne During the Trip to the Swiss Alps)

Stepping out of the town gate at the crack of dawn,

I see morning breezes ruffling the surface of the water.

Boating on the lake surrounded by hills frees my mind,

And I enjoy such secular yet dreamy scenery as if in a fairy

land.

Note: The sky and the earth function separately, but both benefit mankind in their own ways. Mountains nurture life with their kindness, while water nourishes life with its wisdom, so we mortals should never go against nature. Some prefer artificial scenery, while others think natural beauty more appealing. Find yourself a comfort in the world, or you may be lost in nothing to love. Human beings rely on water as the source of life and prosperity; every piece of brick and wood is the gift from nature and for the benefit of life. The breeze rippled the surface of the tranquil lake, and gulls and herons hovered over the verdant banks, as if phoenixes were wheeling in the air and playing with rosy clouds. Such harmony will never end as long as we protect and care for the environment. Switzerland boasts beautiful lakes and lush mountains as well as the buildings which blend in with the surrounding fields, woods and water. We should bear in mind that it was through human's own labor, rather than God's favor, that this great world has been created. Strolling around the lakeshore with a bottle of wine, I immersed myself in an exotic atmosphere.

四 匆匆比利时

Belgium at a Glance

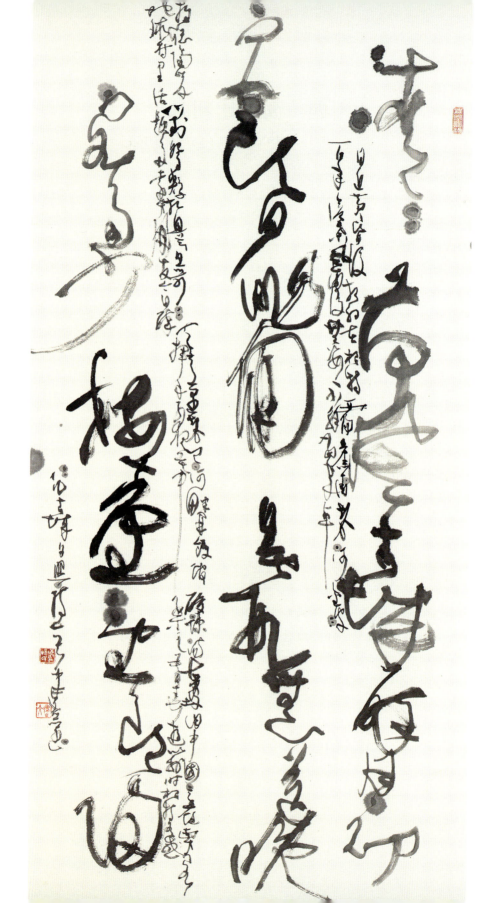

古城夕照

（游比利时古城根特有感）

清清荷风古城醉，月初宫头日徘徊。

夕霞无心送晚客，多少楼台望郎归。

注：日近黄昏后，相约在根特，西阳旧街，老河金波，百年沧桑风雨后，丰姿不解当年卓，推窗隔岸对鸳鸯，相思梦哥哥。无意遇老乡，河畔开饭馆，酸辣汤、东坡肉，中国烹饪西方客。地球村里话题多，远方朋友今日醉，挥手别夜幕。

Ghent at Twilight

The sun, intoxicated by the faint breeze,

Tries to delay its departure as nightfall beckons.

Not even the glorious twilight can prevent the reunion

As man return home to their awaiting loved ones after a long

day.

Note: I recently visited an old street in Ghent, a ravishing Belgian town with hundreds of years of history. While watching lovebirds cavorting in the glistening river, I was reminded of my beloved. Shortly thereafter, I unexpectedly came across a fellow countryman from my home village who managed a riverside Chinese restaurant. I was received warmly by fine wine and the traditional Chinese dishes popular among his western guests. We were so excited to meet in a foreign town on the other side of the world that we did not say goodbye until late that evening.

凡人匠心

（比利时古城市布鲁日印象）

轻輂淡写古城行，水列星空纵波庭。

闲庭不觉瑶池误，雀呼凡尘独匠心。

注：比利时，布鲁日，欧洲兴盛百年磨。且回首，古堡教堂旧钟声，船开街道泛星河，绿云尽头宿白鹭，窗下听船歌。地球本荒原，市井何人落。雕宫琼楼出洞穴，玉辂垂轮理同辙，向前看，文明进化尽智慧，人文艺术和。

Bruges First Impressions

Trip to the ancient town a light touch,

Water sparkling with starry night,

I row in the garden of waves.

Idling wastes not this jade pool,

If in sheer delight of ingenuity

unique to the ordinary.

Note: Bruges of Belgium has instantiated Europe's flourishing for over a century. Looking back, old church bells were chiming as always. Boat floating on the river of stars, egrets resting at the end of greenish clouds, I heard the barcarolle outside the window. Earth was once home to no one, then from whose hands descended towns that we live today? Even magnificent palaces are carved out of caves, and a jade chariot would also leave the same trails. Looking ahead, the evolution of civilization is all about human wisdom harmonizing with art.

五 一个缘

The Call of Destiny

一个缘

（于中国美术学院举办个人书法展之前夜）

苏堤桃花映春晓，钱塘桂子共秋潮。

笑兮红尘一缘字，缘满残雪复断桥。

注：孩时记忆，省城是那么神秘而遥远。雷峰塔下，飞来峰前，演绎了多少天堂故事；西子湖畔，断桥堤边，千年之约，人仙之会依稀间，一个缘。半个世纪后今天，中国美院办个展，五湖四海，朋友相聚，热闹西湖春光无限。俗话说得好，宴席再长也有散；午夜钟声，独自徘徊，思绪万千。看山水静处，光碎冰轮，孤影银发光阴叹，听奶奶讲省城故事，仿佛在昨天。

The Call of Destiny

Springtime is decorated by peach blossoms at the Su Causeway.
Osmanthus flowers witness the autumn tide of the Qiantang
River.
I came to answer the irresistible call of destiny.
So powerful it is, that no broken bridge could keep me away.

Note: I remember my hometown of Hangzhou, Zhejiang as a magnificent wonderland. So many fairy tales stem from there. For example, the story of the Leifeng Pagoda and the Peak Flown From Afar. Most memorable is the story about the bank of the West Lake, where a fairy and a man promised to meet on the Broken Bridge one thousand years later. That tale gave me an idea of what destiny really is. Half a century later, my personal calligraphy exhibition is opening at the China Academy of Art near the same lake. It is as if destiny's call has brought my friends together from all over the country to spend time and enjoy the beautiful spring together. Yet as the saying goes, "all good things must come to an end." Now, in the middle of the night, I am wandering around with all these thoughts and memories. Looking at the lake, I see the light reflecting off the water and it reminds me of my grandmother's silver hair. I can almost hear her telling me the ancient tales of this city.

六　杂弹

Some Sidelights

复兴

天道四时物衰盛，盛世事人汉唐本。
丧权清宫难回首，巍然中华复兴门。

On the Chinese Rejuvenation

All things have their ups and downs as if destined by nature,
But only in the prosperous periods such as Han and Tang
dynasties were people in mirth.
The disgraceful Qing regime had lost its sovereignty and future,
But the Chinese nation is now on a rejuvenating path.

六艺

丹青诗赋小道矣，兴国齐家重教仪。
君子立身修其本，天下太平化六艺。

On the Six Arts*

Calligraphy, painting, poetry and prose are not to mention,
When it comes to thriving home and nation with education and
law.
A noble gentleman would first arm himself with moral
standards to achieve his ambition,
While the six arts are the endowment of a world free of war.

* Translator's note: Six Arts are a set of Confusion-based philosophy
consisting of six disciplines, namely, rites, music, archery, charioting,
calligraphy and mathematics.

38

求实

乾坤曲直藏实虚，左右逢源化心雨。
无悔人生对弈路，落子求实掌险夷。

Truth-seeking

In the infinite universe coexist the right and the wrong, and the
true and the false,
It is by practicing prudence that I have eventually secured my
quest, like there falls a timely rain quenching the drought in my
heart.
For me life is like a game of chess, where I hold no regrets for all
the pieces I lose,
Because only through such practicing and losing will I have a
true insight to tell danger and safety apart.

40

神武

太公八十统军帐，帷幄千里论子房。
悠悠华夏万载兴，文武之道品驰张。

On Military Might

At the age of 80 the Great Duke Jiang Ziya* sat in his military
camp commanding his forces,
While staying hundreds of miles away from the frontline,
Zhang Liang* was able to make precise judgements and give
right commands to the Han troops.
For thousands of years military generals like Jiang and Zhang
served the thriving Chinese nation,
Their doings and achievements left to the comments of later
generations.

* Translator's note: Duke Jiang Ziya and Zhang Liang were two of the
greatest military strategists in ancient China.

家

生命亘古欢天下，人海茫茫家连家。
男儿铁肩女扶持，国泰民安和为大。

Family

Life, for us and the ancients, is all about the pleasure of
travelling.
Wandering in a sea of people, we are connected family by
family.
A man is strong, but stronger when supported by a woman.
Families in harmony, the country peaceful and plenty.

44

福

东海扶桑红，同船连理梦。
平安多幸福，家和天伦共。

Blessing

The red sun rises from the vast East Sea,
Shining on the shared dream of fraternity.
Blessings are bestowed on countries turmoil-free,
Where people indulge themselves in family felicity.

禄

人凡命各殊，无须论贫富。

利禄身外事，寡欲乐知足。

Fortune

Mortals are born with different destinies, so
One shall not be judged by his possession.
When one is old, fortune and status away will go.
While less desire brings far more satisfaction.

寿

昆仑紫霞宫，凌云太极松。
松高笑霜雪，寿齐南山峰。

Longevity

In the sacred Kunlun Mountains and the Zixia Palace,
The pine trees in the fog stand like Tai Chi masters.
Standing proudly against the frost and snow's malice,
They live up to the Zhongnan Mountains' long years.

禅

禅者言佛形，无心玄藏经。
人生多苦难，菩提众生引。

Zen

Zen practitioners talk about Buddha's form,
Not to emphasize the knowledge of sutras and doctrines.
For all, sufferings and struggles in life are the norm,
It is Bodhi that enlightens and guides all humans.

悟

生命贵贱无，智巧潜灵府。
持之终能成，游刃真谛悟。

Enlightenment

All lives are equal regardless of their birth,
And the differences lie in the thoughts in their brains.
Perseverance will finally contribute to one's worth,
Bear that in mind, epiphany will be gained with no pains.

静

白浪唱黄河，无意楚汉歌。
不息旧时水，静心听今波。

Serenity

The flashing waves chant the roars of the Yellow River,
Leaving behind the ancient bellowing strife between the great
kings.*
The water keeps running regardless of what time has to deliver,
And I am attentively listening to what now the river sings.

* Translator's note: The great kings here refer to Liu Bang, the
founding emperor of the Han dynasty (206 BC–220 AD) and
Xiang Yu, once a great rival of Liu Bang.

觉

有色视物形，无声相物心。
空明灵府觉，宇宙藏心镜。

Awakening

In form you see only the appearance, the being,
but in silence, you feel the mind, the thinking.
Empty, clear, will your home of spirit be awakened,
that universe secrets itself here within, the mind-mirror.

春雨

九尽野陌东，夜雷惊寒空。
一年好收成，濛濛春雨中。

Spring Rain

Through the cold sky, the night thunder rumbles,
Signaling the end of winter and the start of spring.
The drizzling spring rain mumbles,
About a good and bumper year it will surely bring.

秋华

春水溢夏渠，细流从长计。
待到月盈潮，秋华红霞倚。

Autumn Blossoms

In spring the water runs and in summer it brims in the ditches,
For a smaller volume of stream ensures a longer flow.
When the moon is full and tides rise over the beaches,
Against the sunset clouds the autumn blossoms glow.

寒梅

春艳百花台，疏影孤寒梅。

遥望君子步，不言苦为谁。

The Winter Plum

In the spring the world shines with hundreds of flowers,
But now the winter plum, casting a shadow, blossoms alone.
From afar it is appreciated by admirers,
But how bitter of the coldness will never be known.

苦读

人生仕浮图，智知书山路。
苦读孤寒窗，金榜花烛赋。

Study Hard

Prosperity of life is a stupa,

And a wise man knows the way.

Studying night after night in his chilling shanty,

Then he will succeed and find his bride.

勤勉

世事江海篇，片舟夜航艰。
迟恐有风浪，勤勉意更坚。

Diligence

Life is sailing on the sea, or a river great,
A tiny craft steering hard at night.
Don't hesitate — a storm may come at any time,
And diligence will make your will stronger.

花香

东风何时归，江暖柳色微。
草深庭院梦，花香恋蝶醉。

Fragrance of Flowers

When will easterly wind blow again?
River water warms and willow leaves sprout.
I lie in my thriving backyard dreaming,
Lost in the fragrance of flowers and ballet of butterflies.

太极

起手丹田云复雨，天地之大五常居。

轮回日月对两端，吐故阴阳运太极。

Tai Chi

Lightly, the arms curve upward,

Slowly, breathe from the lower elixir field.

Hands are drawn like cloud going with wind.

The world is as infinite as people say,

But the five virtues will always stay.

At the break of the day,

The rising sun and the setting moon appear in the same sky.

Exhale the past foul air and Tai Chi is the thing you should play,

At the time when the complementary forces of yin and yang lie.

60

起舞

四时三春好，朝菌叹暮潮。
闻鸡勤五更，起舞歌白少。

Work Hard

Of four seasons spring is the prime,
Ah, but short like a morning mushroom's life.
The tide of dusk rising, make full use of your time,
And work hard when your hair is still dark.

62

四海

四海苍茫无疆土，五洲桑田绽新图。

七夕星际云和月，天涯何处朋友孤。

The Four Seas

The Four Seas are so vast that no one sees their boundaries.

And across the Five Continents new sceneries are forming

in the fields that have witnessed shifting sceneries.

At this night when through the clouds the same moon is
roaming,

In the same sky by scattered stars dimly shone.

Wherever you are, my friend, you shall not be alone.

潮声

光阴无边四时分，江河纵横列乾门。

欣然潮起看潮落，临风波头辨潮声。

The Tide Sounds

Time, though endless, is divided into four seasons.

And all the rivers run southeast for nature's reasons.

Standing in the wind, I watch the tides rise and fall,

To first hear the magnificent sounds of the tide wall.

66

长城

不尽黄水千年波，一曲长城风雪和。
凡尘悠悠望不及，青峰岭上正气歌。

The Great Wall

For thousands of years, the water of the Yellow River runs on
and on,
Accompanied by wind and snow, the Great Wall stands all
along.
The infinity of the world is more than I can ponder upon,
So I climb up the Qingfeng Mountain, and recite the
Righteousness Song.

积善

风霜雪雨天地事，红尘普度学而智。
智仁天下勤当孝，积善修德功世嗣。

To Accumulate Virtues

Be it windy, rainy, frosty or snowy, weather is a thing of nature.
While to salvage others is the ultimate knowledge and wisdom
for humans.
Diligence and filial piety are what every wise and humane
person summons,
So that the merits and virtues will benefit the generations in the
future.

70

余庆

金风十月喜秋果，百年树人一年谷。
泉盈点滴恩泽心，家有余庆幸福多。

The Bountiful Harvest

In the breeze of October, the autumn fruits hang on the trees,
The crops take a year to grow, but a person to be an expertise
Needs almost a hundred years of hard training.
A fountain stays full because it collects water when it's raining,
While a family with bountiful harvest is where happiness is
shining.

农桑

洛阳水席满汉宴，衣食农桑百姓田。
闲来琼楼空对月，笑问王孙自可怜。

Farming and Sericulture

The rich feast on the water banquet in Luoyang, which is plush
and grand,
While their food and clothes come from farmers growing
mulberries and tilling the land.
Mounting the magnificent building, alone with the moon I
stand,
To wonder whether the rich would pity themselves in the end.

七 天山来客

A Visit to Mount Tianshan

从赛里木湖过果子沟

六月西域沐西风，风轻波谷步山重。
山里光阴问长短，四季一宿朝暮中。

注：自博乐至赛果木湖，无意坡陡路途，欢声笑语随白云。不觉山高藏平湖。湖光波滟，长天透碧，雪山倒影，群峰盼顾，美景更待云深处。过山门，攀峰岩，沟壑纵横步天堑。寒气逼，袭单衣，朝暮四季难分辨，忘却老身何图。

From Sayram Lake to Fruit Valley

In June, I was bathed in the wind of the Western Regions,
Walked through the mountains in the wind-swept valley.
In the nature, it's hard to tell the time,
It seemed that the change of season happened overnight.

Note: During the trip from Bole to Sayram Lake. I have no intention of taking a steep and dangerous road, and I walked with my friends all the way under the white clouds with joy and laughter. Along the way, mountains are beautiful, and the lake was tranquil and glazing. The clear water reflected blue sky and snow mountains. Breath-taking scenery hid in the depth of white clouds. I passed the mountain gate and climbed the rock, through the ravines. It's bitterly cold. I was puzzled, it's hard to distinguish the day and night, and seasons. I even forgot who I am, and what I'm longing for.

昭苏牧歌

草天茫茫依太虚，晨曦一线苏紫衢。
唯看天边鱼肚色，东方既白饮马曲。

注：踏晨风，出发昭苏，扬鞭纵马，翠色千里，一路紫气云舒。心地怦然，勒马饮川远眺，如此美景谁赐。天边有石人，不知何时静立，欲近前，问身世，尽低头，唯听草浪声楚。

Pastoral Life in Zhaosu County

The extensive grassland reaches to the skyline,
With morning glory waking up the sleeping lane.
In the dawn, the sky is as bright as the fish's belly,
It's the beginning of the day, so call the horses to drink.

Note: In the morning breeze, we were heading to Zhaosu County. I cracked the whip and the horse leapt forward. All I saw was extensive green scenery, and the weather was pleasant with cloud drifting in the air. I was amazed by what I saw, so I stopped the horse and took a look at the distance. Nature! There was a human-shaped stone standing in the distance. No one knows when did it stand over there. I tried to reach it and find out who it is and why he was there, but I didn't get any response. The world was so silent that I barely hear the sound of wind in the grassland.

古道吟

（步夏塔古道）

一

春花秋月数光阴，请君一曲古道情。

置身烈日追飞雪，回首辄逍凝古今。

二

绿山、黄山复紫山，青杉白杨数红杉。

湍飞一朵天际乱，惊虹临坡古道长。

注：夏日长，古道忙，翻山涉水岗连岗，古道漫漫通古今，光阴流水消途。才说骄阳酷，瞬时西风勤，雪花舞乱天六月，风云难测。登高处，见远影，隐隐张骞持节，牧羊苏武。观雪山静立，不知夏暑，奈何！奈何！

Walking on an Ancient Path

I

How time flies! The spring blossoms and the moon of autumn.
Please, play that ancient ode.
Being in the sizzling sun, I reflected the snowy winter,
On looking back, I saw the miniature of history.

II

Colorful mountains, green, yellow, and purple mountains.
Green trees — aspens, and numerous redwoods on the way.
The rushing rivers broke the skyline,
A rainbow was hanging on the slope, the long road stretched
into the distance.

Note: In the long summer, there were many tourists in this place. We waded the mountains and rivers to experience the old path. How time flies! The path tells many stories. Fickle weather! The sizzling summer was overwhelmed by cool west wind. In June, it felt like winter. I ascended to a height and had a look. At a distance, I saw some vague figures. I thought about some historic figures who went to western regions to protect their country. I watched the snowy mountain and contemplated for a long time. I even forgot it was summer!

相约那拉提

长空无垠纵翠色，岗石零乱芳草涯。

遥看牧童驰天堑，醉卧西风斜阳下。

注：眼前花坡锦田，身后群峰绵绵，美景尽在山深处，遥指牧童没林渚。林密密，涧无数，千迴百折望不及，芳草荡碧弧。牛羊牧草在天头，牧童越马纵鸿沟。愿君纵情唱一曲，意犹兴，夕阳淡，云生处，崖断忘却归路。

In Nalati

Under the endless sky was full of emerald green,

Among the grass, the rocks were messy.

At the distance, a shepherd was riding freely,

I would like to be drunk and laid down in the sunset.

West wind was blowing.

Note: In front of us, flower field stretched to the slope. The beauty is hidden deep in the mountains stretching behind. The shepherd's figure was lost in the forests. Deep in the forests, there were numerous streams. The winding streams had no end in sight, only the grass was blown out of the blue waves by the wind. The shepherd boy rode across the gully only for the distant pasture. Please indulge in singing! We were in good mood. In the faded sunset, we walked to a cliff hid in the clouds and had no idea how to return.

天山观天池

山高水深说灵名，试足群峰天山临。

云深犹闻众神语，探身瑶池辨仙音。

注：天山高，天山远，天山在天上，不知天路长何许，尽情随云意。云层层，风萧萧，览胜景，寻径仙乐，直上月宫向嫦娥，瑶池何去？只道瑶池有美酒，仙界探妙奇，心欲重，难拒。嘻嘻！人好高走，高处不胜寒，能舍红尘依依。

In Tianchi of Mount Tianshan

In China, majestic mountains and waters are interpreted as
deities.
Among these gorgeous mountains, Mount Tianshan must be a
top-notch one.
Deep in the clouds, I could hear some god-like voice,
I turned to a holy lake to find whereabouts of gods.

Note: Mount Tianshan is far away. It's hard to tell the right path, just follow the drifting clouds. I was lost in the divine clouds and blowing wind. What a breath-taking scenery! I hoped that I could go to the moon palace to find some goddess. Where are they? Where is the Yaochi — the divine palace of the queen of heaven? People say that there are good wine in Yaochi. It's hard to resist the temptation for human beings. Alas! We all aspire something big, yet few can know the price. Being a god means that you need to cut off all the ties with the secular world.

罗布人家

白云、黄云浑无路，红柳依依悟沙途。

天边悠悠驼铃响，胡杨深处纵罗布。

注：胡杨、胡杨，沙漠骄子，生存毅力，横目千里，黄云白日乱头绪。直面骄阳无情，仰首长空，骄阳何以解话题。常言道，万物生长靠太阳，苦骄阳太狠，无言自欺。好也太阳，苦亦太阳，地球家园，绝处庭落，胡杨依然，亘古记忆。

A Trip to Luobu People's Hometown

During the trip, clouds were yellowed by sandstorm,

These rose willows stood along the road.

We heard the sound of camel bells in the distance,

In the depth of Populus euphratica forestsm,

Luobu people pursued a tranquil life.

Note: Populus euphratica can endure drought of desert. Its tenacious vitality lasts forever under the dire weather condition. Populus euphratica bravely faces the dazzling sun, and all the challenges. All the living creatures in the Nature rely on sunshine. But sunshine can also make life suffer. The earth witnesses numerous changes throughout history, and the Populus euphratica seems to be immortal.

草甸黄昏随想

（巴音布鲁克观日落）

纵马登高古原醉，飞霞随云草色微。

扬鞭九曲尽西去，仰天笑问何处归。

注：还说天堂好，可比人间美，奔波千里赏美景，道不完，只为那一瞥。时六月，正值新疆游乐季，游人如织，蜂拥一地，欣然草原深处。草原那头有何奇？心疑。无须问，纵情意，穿芳甸，绕水口，略五霞，上高台，凭栏远眺，黄昏已。美景只等这一刻，草色惊落薄阳，随金色曲尽西。来也匆匆，去也匆匆，苦别离。

Prairie at Dusk

On the horseback I visit the prairie,

Under the floating sunset clouds the grass is glittering.

Along the meandering river I ride west,

Lean back and wonder, where is my nest.

Note: The heaven on earth is truly beautiful. I travelled thousands of miles, only for a glance of her beauty. It was June, the prime season for touring the prairie. The crowds jostled each other, just as a swarm of bees bustled in the grass. I could not help wondering, what was beyond the prairie? Ha. No need to ask. To my heart's content, I traversed the prairie, passed by rivers, appreciated the glowing sunsets, ascended a tower and overlooked the spectacular view. Soon, the dusk came. I waited so long a time, for only a moment of such fine view. The golden sunset shed on the grass, edging down in the west. In a hurry I came. In haste, I went back. Mirthless it was to leave such beauty behind.

八 故乡云
Where I Belong

花儿为谁红

（故乡上溪观十里桃花坞赏花有感）

桃花粉、李花浓，桃李无言笑春风。

风醒溪路水有声，峰回山柳沾花红。

注：山桃笑春风，高楼问梧桐。已是暮春三月后，为何不见燕子来堂中。水恋故乡美，山情故乡浓，山花细雨泥泞路，渔塘水车老屋唱牧童。

A Sea of Pink

The peach and prunus blossoms are in full bloom,
Shining brightly and smiling in the spring breeze.
The meadows sway with the breeze along the winding stream.
Rosy hills covered by a sea of pink.

Note: The peach blossoms dance in the spring breeze and the Phoenix trees have grown and now tower over my house. It's already March, but why haven't the swallows started to visit? What a shame! I love my beautiful hometown of Shangxi. Flower pedals dance in the drizzle along the muddy paths. A shepherd boy sings in front of an old house near the waterwheel. It is like a snapshot from a dream!

葵花段子

野径晨曦赶花廊，紫霞茅屋翔金鸾。
纵看人间春色后，新月争空笑骄阳。

注：葵花、葵花，大路天涯。朝东暮西把光景，一心向太阳。太阳普金辉，娇月羞紫霞，盼得花好月圆时，太平天下；话太平，天空有阴晴，大地道不平，凡尘迷离光阴叹，无需伤心。平常态，衷初情，追雷电，沐风雨，不尽人间须欢乐，醉里畅花影。

Sunflower

Morning leads me to a wild path in sunflower corridor,
Above cottages fly golden birds clad in purple glow.
Been through all the springs in the world,
A new moon rises, smiling to the sun.

Note: Sunflower, sunflower, blooms in this land and goes the distance. You follow steps of the sun, facing east at dawn and west at dusk. The sun casts a golden sheen, while the shy moon blushes at the purple glow. Hope when flowers bloom under a full moon, a time of peace and prosperity will come. Talking about peace, however, there is no road always level and no sky always sunny, so you don't need to shed tears for the mystery of time. Just stay normal and go back to what you love. Enjoy your life — chasing the thunder and lightning, bathing in the wind and rain, and wandering in the shadows of flowers while drunk.

绣湖亲亲

（六十年后回故乡办书法展有感）

秋锦波平兴绣湖，话别少年还老夫。
慢步旧堤问古塔，何解人生光阴路。

注：乡愁，乡愁，少年猖狂老儿愁。离乡六十载，背井经风雨，多少往事随浮云，无计少时别离太匆匆，难回头。缘未了，重聚绣湖话当年，人生如戏叹白首，好男儿，志四方，无须伤情，修身，持家，平天下，老骥途犹。

Dear Xiuhu

(Return to Hometown After 60 Years for
My Calligraphy Fair)

I visit serene Xiuhu again in a graceful autumn,
Last time I was here being a teenager, now I'm in my declining
years.
I wander along the ancient dyke, and look at the old pagoda
nearby,
Reflecting on my past time never come back again.

Note: In my old age, homesickness is deeply engrained in my body, melancholy replaced innocence in my prime. I've already left my hometown for 60 years. What I experienced and went through shaped who I am today. Oh! What a pity that I left so hastily and find little chance to return. Luckily, I finally return to my hometown and reunited with my old friends in Xiuhu. We reflected on our past time. Don't be sad! Brave men with great aspirations, no matter how old they are, should focus on self-cultivation, family well-being and the world's prosperity.

残荷词

（访武义郭洞古村有感）

青峰青石山路长，落红败叶暗荷伤。

且随石桥飞天去，秋水泥池待星朗。

注：翻青山，越溪索，古村幽幽依山谷，山水层层展画卷，野陌袅袅绕美田，先民何意深山居，自神仙。神仙好，神仙悠，松风听乱弹。无意水碓空，残荷摇，拽群峰，千岩锁得风光好，难全村郎读书穷。今日匆匆过，难知古人风，山里尽显耕读事，曾经亦从容。

Withered Lotus

(After Visiting Ancient Village in Guodong)

Walking on the steep mountain road surrounded by green
plants and stones,
I saw fallen red leaves and withered lotus.
The long stone bridge extended to the skyline,
A pond full of autumn rain disclosed under the clear night sky,
Stars were looming …

Note: I climbed over the mountains, went across the brooks and finally arrived at the ancient village located in the valley. The beautiful scenery unfolded in front of my eyes, winding roads surrounded fertile lands. Life of the ancients in this remote area must be very happy without pressure. They could hear the sounds of wind going through pine trees. How time flies! Now all you can find is withered lotus. The scenery of mountains is still gorgeous. Sadly, people are too poor to achieve better educations. Time was limited, and I couldn't feel this antique village thoroughly. I could imagine the abundant life in the past through remains of agriculture.

斜阳桥

（访武义山下鲍村有感）

青峰斜阳复山径，野陌草篱掩画庭。

一溪切分两岸石，留得残桥观山景。

注：武义、武义，美景深山里，山深谓穷地，仁智乐山水，武义显仁义。山下鲍，在何处，踏破青山寻古意，心揣祖业索奇想，思成留足迹。志壮怀，追往昔，双双无去向，雕祠低叹息，旧栋横竖尘泥厚，孤风残桥无依，随风雨。

Xieyang Bridge

(After Visiting Bao Village in Wuyi)

The setting sun goes through the ghat hidden in the green hills,

Nature's beauty expresses most in the wild.

A brook flows in the middle of the road,

Only a broken bridge left to see the view in the distance.

Note: Wuyi's beauty can be found in the mountains. Places surrounded by mountains are often regarded as less advantaged areas. Kind and wise men love seeing natural scenery, and in Wuyi I found kindness and wisdom deeply rooted in people's mind. I managed to find the Bao Village at the foot of the hill. I wandered around to find some quaint traces. Later I drew my inspiration for family legacy. At reminiscence of the past, the man with ambitions has long gone with passing time. I signed when seeing the ancient hall. Shabby house was covered with mud; a lonely broken bridge stood in the rain.

鱼儿乐

（访武义俞源太极星象村有感）

秋打芙蓉艳画屏，斜郭青峰镶锦庭。

莫言门前溪水浅，问得鱼儿可安宁。

注：山民思山田，市井忙商计，碌碌一生多少事，忙里偷闲意。人生何是头，看白驹过隙，山里自有山里乐，无须更多，知足便矣！秋风至，闲云寄，纵看溪谷倚栏杆，赏花趣。自得鱼儿乐逆水，尽享时下三分地。太极、太极、人尊天理。

Fish Ode

(After Visiting Yuyuan Tai Chi Star Village in Wuyi)

Gorgeous hibiscus blossom in the autumn,

Magnificent buildings are surrounded by inclined hills.

Fish swim carefreely in the brook in front of the house,

Shallow water also brings satisfaction and joy to fish.

Note: In the villages, farmers think about farming, and in the cities, people focus on business. How can we escape from the hustle and bustle of the life and find some inner peace? How time flies! Those who live in remote areas also feel fulfilled and satisfied. What we have now is the best! In the autumn breeze, I lean on the rail to overlook the valley. I appreciate the beautiful flowers and drifting cloud in the distance. I enjoy this moment at this place, feeling as if I were the fish swimming in the water. This might exactly be the essence of Tai Chi — follow the nature's rules.

拜老道

（访太极村口伯温道院有感）

说刘基、道伯温，旧壁残院拜空真。

有道树大经天地，无为自乐守山门。

注：人相异，道不同，大路朝天随尔走，百年树人知任重。秦汉业，宋唐基，天下春秋数英雄，男儿当自强，将相本无种。今日兴游伯温祠，残阶闲步拜老道，诉夜幕，皓月渐东日归处，静听伯温驾哀鸿。

On Visiting an Ancient Abbey

(Bowen Abbey at the Entry of Tai Chi Star Village)

When talking about Liuji, the renowned politician in the Ming
dynasty,

I can only recall him through dilapidated walls and yards.

A well-learned man can fulfill his ambitions in the life journey,

An ordinary person also feels satisfied by doing nothing and

being the true self.

Note: People are different and have different values and goals. Everyone has the right to choose the best way for themselves. It's such a great mission to nurture virtuous men. The glory of the Qin and Han dynasties, and the cultural legacy in the Tang and Song dynasties were made by many heroes in the era. Diligent men can achieve their ambitions regardless of family backgrounds. I visited Bowen Abbey this day. I walked on the dilapidated steps at night, and watched the moon moving to the east. Bowen's soul is drifting in the air, just like crying geese.

背影

（访武义银坑古村有感）

山空松影抱斜阳，横溪秋稿迷路向。

寻声林密复青苔，背妇夕霞渐西岗。

注：人处何时说何话，行身山地陌路把，山路弯弯多险处，辨足下。人何能，易乾坤，翻云覆雨诣上苍，无须劳心思，人生本已多苦难，无苦不甜对月觞，温室花儿不长久，纵看践草飞扬。话虽山里多单调，败蝉蛙田修心房，听得鸡鸣犬吠时，享尽清风明月，何干！

A Figure

(After Visiting Yinkeng Village in Wuyi)

In the silent mountain, shadows of pine trees are seen clearly in the setting sun,

I get lost in the mountain where brooks splitting the road.

Autumn is always bleak, and I manage to find the sounds through dense trees and moss.

A woman passes by with a basket carried on the back.

The setting sun is moving to the west peak.

Note: In different situations, we must think differently. When walking on the unfamiliar mountain, we must be more careful about the dangerous road. People have limited power. It's impossible to change the world and the nature. Life is already hard, one can propose a toast to the moon and show your happiness and sadness. People can grow up through experiencing difficulties. Though living in the mountain is dull and simple, but you can hear different songs: cicadas' chirping, fog's noises, roosters and dogs … You can also enjoy the breeze and beautiful moon!

秋田赋

（游武义花田小镇有感）

西霞霜风秋菊黄，东田花径话农桑。

正值江南稻谷好，此处农家不思粮。

注：骄阳空，秋无意，西风虽已过江南，黄叶地。无心赏景致，花田弄锦绣，娇态故作无限思，匆匆步履。陌田花季，游人络绎，娇然倾城惹闲汉，霜风催尽颜去。无奈祖辈良田竞谁主，残阳尽落钱孔里。

Field in the Fall

(After Visiting an Idyllic Country in Wuyi)

Chrysanthemums blossom in the frost wind.

Under the western sunset, we chat about farmland in the east
field.

In the regions of the Yangtze River, rice yield is very ideal,

So here families don't have to worry about food.

Note: Sizzling season has gone, autumn brings about cold wind from the west to southern regions. Fallen leaves laying on the ground. I'm not in the mood for sightseeing. Flowers blossom in the field, but I'm too busy to savor these beautiful things. The field is full of visitors in the blossom season. People woo the beauty, but frost wind can quickly destroy it. From generation to generation, every owner pursues money, the only thing that never changes is the sunset.

九　滇南行

A Tour in South Yunnan Province

蛮地荷影

（游云南普者黑万亩荷田有感）

千峰百折复长水，绿荷遥天众香随。

花深径底忘归路，一鸟惊波笑莲台。

注：诸葛渡泸水，孟获居蛮宫，千年戏文唱故人，是非多少回。叹昔时，南蛮地，蛮荒雨林瘴气重，人迹罕至，鸟不飞；难尽陈年事，直名普者黑，物换人非。如今光阴正提速，同一山，同一水，网红人鼎沸。

Lotus Field in Puzhehei

I flew over a thousand mountains,

To a place where green lotus leaves spread over to the horizon.

Surrounded by lotus flowers, I forgot my way back as I roamed around,

When suddenly a bird flitted and made the lotus nod in the pond.

Note: Yunnan is the place where Zhuge Liang of Shu Han (221–263 AD) put down a rebellion staged by the local tribal chief Meng Huo. This story has been written into plays and performed on stage for nearly two thousand years, and has received both appreciations and critics. Yunnan was once called the southern barbarian frontier, where thick rain forests and poisonous miasma kept outsiders from entering, and even birds dared not fly pass. But what's past is past, and I'm now in the scenic village of Puzhehei, where the trace of Yunnan's undeveloped times could not be found. The mountains and lakes stay the same, but this place is no longer a waste land — countless travellers come to visit for its good reputation online.

清浊花

（普者黑五女羞芙蓉）

青荷无穷望碧霞，一镜幽水瑶台下。

移步探峰照妾脸，玉指弹波羞万花。

注：人之初，性本善，善美正莲台，莲台落尘世，尘封叹泥埃。原本楚楚冰洁身，洁身好自为；泥污浊，水尚清，清浊两难开，丽日徐风待花日，芙蓉沐初水。水形天娇虚心处，灵府透碧彩。

Lotus

(Five Beautiful Girls from Puzhehei)

Bondless green lotus leaves look up to the blue sky,

The pond, like a mirror, reflects this heavenly sight.

Walking in the hill nearby, I saw five local girls

playing by the water,

Dabbling their hands, their grace

envied by the blooming lotus flowers.

Note: It is said that Buddha sits on a lotus blossom, the symbol of kindness and stainless beauty. Now I am surrounded by a pond of lotus flowers, but unlike in Buddhist stories, they rise from earthly slimy mud. Luckily, the water is clear, and these heavenly flowers repose modestly on the pond, pure and taintless. I can imagine that sometime in the next coming days, when the sun is bright and the breeze is warm, the lotus buds would all turn into full blooms. Thanks to the clear water that flows through their stems, and the mud nourishing their roots, they would look as stunning as they were in Buddhist heavens, with beauty that is unparalleled on earth.

撒尼花

（普者黑赶市）

普者黑、黑云霞，一隅红土撒尼花。

花黑幽然待尔觅，冷箭孤傲怒天涯。

注：七月赶盛夏，普者观黑霞，悠然荷塘探深处，江洲骄阳把。一方水土一方人，人勤天长，虽普天下太阳共有，唯此处好，逝水流华。守住太阳，娇艳撒尼眸，万物皆感光景好，无悔黑透。

Ode to the Sani Minority

Unparalleled in Puzhehei is the magnificent evening glow, while
On this beautiful land of red soil live the Sani people. Of whom,
The girls have unique beauty with their dark skin color, and the lads,
Who have extraordinary archery skills, are worthy of the name
of best warriors among their peers.

Note: In midsummer in July I come to Puzhehei to appreciate its well-known sunset and evening clouds. This village of boundless lotus field has a lot of sunny days throughout the year, thus the local people of the Sani Minority, *usually have dark skin color due to a lot of sun exposure.

* Sani Minority: a branch of the Yi Minority in southwest China.

异乡魂

（夜宿抚仙湖）

银滩白浪浸西霞，鸳鸯对对归寒沙。

沙暖初月伴异客，星光微处又一家。

注：赶路，赶路，夕阳坠闲洲渚。已是星火点点晦晚岸，湖光依然楚楚；看闲客人涌，游兴方艾，摇旗埋头寻深巷，不知今宵何处。

A Night by Fuxian Lake

In the sunset are the silver beach and waves glittering.

Side by side the mandarin ducks return to their nest.

With no company but the crescent moon and stars shimmering,

I see yet another home for somebody else to rest.

Note: When I was heading for my next destination one evening, I saw, by the Fuxian Lake, the sun sinking below the horizon beyond the water, and the moonlight on the lake outshining stars and household lights. As the lakeside was by then crowded with tourists, I felt not lingering around any longer. So I took a path less travelled, and went on my journey, knowing not where it would end that night.

归渡

（抚仙湖之今昔随想）

西阳镜渡待前川，纵波一线水连天。

飞霞朵朵白帆近，闻歌浪头归渔船。

注：此地本渔村，偏僻舟相问，片片渔舟唱晚风，随浪泊家门；归渡，归渡，如今酒楼商铺，晚风回眸浪已静，雕车宝马骧路。

Fishing Boats Returning Home

The setting sun admires its reflection in the lake,

And the water runs towards the horizon.

The clouds drift in the twilight far away,

Shadowing dozens of white sails returning.

Along with a wave, a brisk melody comes this way,

Followed by the singing fishermen with their harvest of the day.

Note: Here it was once an isolated village, that could only be visited by boats. The villagers made a living on fishing, who were, in the evening breeze, sent home by tender waves. Now the tranquility is long gone, but a busy town crowded with visitors and stores stands. Cars can be seen everywhere on the streets, only the water and breeze remain as they were in the old days.

一个问

（城子古村之当代畅想）

六百春秋说短长，物非星移几寒霜。
樑旧思燕故巢在，漠然新人淡乡愁。

注：农家地，荒山里，四季风雨勤耕作，一年收成低；思生命，为何苦，弃农田，寻出息。稻米只能足温饱，灯红酒绿好滋味。快哉，快哉，哪有生命离农计。

Thoughts on the Ancient Village of Chengzi

Through six centuries of rise and fall the houses stand.
Swallow nests await on beams, but their owners never return —
Young sons and daughters have long left for an opportunity land.
"Hometown" is merely a simple noun no more their concern.

Note: On the poor soil between the barren hills, no hard work can get a bumper harvest. Why labor hard when it can never pay the bills? Leave the farmland, and you can find what is best. Why struggle farming to make ends meet, when there is an affluent life waiting in the cities? How happy urban life is! But how could it last when all farmers have left the fields?

十　婺源赏青

Enjoying the Spring in Wuyuan

柳枝词

（游婺源严田村）

东风二月春来早，随君赏花意恐迟。
林径忽闻前朝曲，今人不解杨柳枝。

注：菜花田，桃柳陌，粉墙黑瓦望溪水。水轻婉转斜山雨，溪桥静候牧童归。六姨太，显达贵，人去楼空照井台。台高古今异戏文，村口古樟翻新牌。

Willow Twig Song

(A Tour to Yantian Village in Wuyuan)

The east wind in February brought spring here early,
Rushing us to go for a trip to enjoy the floral season.
Suddenly I heard a cliche tune from the past dynasty played in
the lane of forest,
Leaving me lost in the original "Willow Twig Song".

Note: By the field of cauliflowers and the lane of peach blossoms and willows, the spring water flows through the buildings featuring white walls and black-tile roofs. Rain falling, the bridge stands still over the river, waiting for the return of the farmer boy. This noble family once owned six concubines. However, what is now left is nothing but an empty well. Different shows in different times. The old camphora of the village now hangs a new brand.

东风解

（夜宿婺源丛溪庄园）

几重青山几度空，粉面桃花两濛濛。

东风柳色年年似，昨夜春梦何不同。

注：久闻婺源胜景，今春如愿其境。丛溪庄园，坐落于婺源市郊，原来一片良田。其仿徽州古风，甚是气派。高墙深院，依山傍水，田原中显出几分豪迈，吸引着八方闲客前来。大江南北，大兴土木。其实，这样的庄园比比皆是，而今晚又能睡出个什么别样风味。

The Song of Easterly Winds

(A Night at Congxi Manor in Wuyuan)

Green mountains empty,

Peach blossoms boom in a drizzle.

Easterly winds blow the same willows,

But last night why a different dream I expected.

Note: I have heard the name of the breathtaking scenery of Wuyuan for long and finally I realized my dream this spring. The Congxi Manor, located in the suburb of Wuyuan, used to be a fertile cropland. Near a river and by the mountain, the Hui-Style manor was grand and exquisite, attracting visitors from all over the country. Now that such manors have been built everywhere, I wondered what a different dream I would have tonight.

菜花调

（游婺源观江岭梯田油菜花）

晨开薄雾踏清风，岫云蝶径上九重。

闲作一日江岭客，醉看黄花娇天空。

注：婺源之美，尽显菜花本色。菜花美婺源，最美在江岭，蜿蜒崇山花随风，昏昏入仙境。香气沁心，黄金陌路，彩蝶招引，忽闻鸡鸣犬吠，凝望碧空，尽止于青绿黄蓝，霓裳倩影。

Song of Cauliflowers

The mist of dawn is carried by the wind,

Wound up to the sky along with the cloud.

Travelling in Jiangling,

I was drown in the yellow flowers and the pure sky.

Note: Cauliflowers are the symbol of Wuyuan, of which the most beautiful are in Jiangling. Like a paradise, vast fields of flowers scatter over the mountain, the fragrance of which in the air. The fragrance reached deep in my heart and drew the butterflies near. Suddenly I heard the cries of chickens and dogs and looked up to the blue sky. I saw only radiant colors glowing in front of me.

梨花春寒

（游婺源江湾村过梨院）

南墙高楼戏台静，北巷梨院花珠阴。

东风犹早雨未湿，梨花争春一夜馨。

注：平平江湾村，今日兴游人。高墙岁痕，老屋苍陈。残垣深处藏龙脉，寻得野草孤门。后院几株梨，随君漫步移，今日尚春早，花珠待枝倚。四时光景日日好，好花尚能百日迷，终落得世人叹息。

Pear Blossom in the Cold Spring
(A Trip to Jiangwan Village in Wuyuan)

No sound on the high stage in the south,

Pear blossom shading over the lane in the north,

East wind has yet to come and the print of rain still remains,

Fragrance of flowers lingers overnight.

Note: The humble Jiangwan Village is now crowded with tourists. High buildings and old cottages are weathered in ages. I searched for the dragon vein in the depths of dilapidated walls, only to find weeds and houses in ruins. I walked around the pear trees in the backyard. The flowers are still blossoming as the spring has yet to come. Yet the flourishing can only last for a season. I sighed with regret.

商海沉浮

（访思溪村有感）

梨花一枝素青郭，数叶垂丝乱春波。

波尽鸬鹚水深处，惊叹商海往事多。

注：公主阁，姨太房，重楼高闺过了墙。商重利，义不忘，墙角处处去棱角，遵循祖法礼三让。时过境迁，商号不再，游人扬长，移步青石听往事，留下的是思量。

Drifting in the Wild Sea of Business

(Thoughts on Visiting Sixi Village)

A twig of white pear blossom reached across the blue wall,

Hanging leaves crept over the water.

I walked down toward the end of the river,

Marveling about the past stories of the business world.

Note: The boudoirs of ladies and chambers of mistresses are hidden beyond the wall. A businessman's family still values integrity. Corners are smooth. Politeness are recommended. Circumstances change with the passage of time. The family is here no more, replaced by endless lines of tourists. I stepped aside to the green stones, wondering about the past tales.

徽宅门

（访婺源延村有感）

古村虽老风骨存，菜花犹新望残门。

回首断垣江南绝，叹哉东风寄重生。

注：高山青，溪水长，野田禾苗土芳香。环村四周皆泥土，不知何人思从商。人皆知，欲何奈。富不过三代，穷又何样。当年气魂早不存，回首残壁瓦砾场。新房总比旧屋好？雕楼飘摇，好不痛心肠。

The Gate of a Hui-style House

(Thoughts on the Yan Village in Wuyuan)

The village aged yet style remains,

Bright rapeseeds flowering at the shabby gate.

Looking back on dilapidated houses century-old,

How I wish easterly winds bring them back to life.

Note: Mountains green and streams gurgling, the village surrounded by paddy fields was heavy with the aroma of rice seedlings. I wondered why villagers wanted to do business in a city — wealth cannot be held for more than three generations, but poverty is not unbearable. They used to value the rustic lifestyle, but houses they lived are dilapidated now. Why did people think new houses were better than old ones? Seeing the wooden buildings with carvings worn out, my heart was aching.

篁岭春色

（婺源最美乡村篁岭有感）

古木林深不知处，山抱峰回望梨树。

梨花彩墨粉墙动，青阶尽头读春书。

注：步坡街，通幽径，世外桃源说山民。山中自有山中语：时下山民衷市井。闲客只道赏花景，可知山劳多辛勤。春雨油，汗下土，收成全靠天上助。天人合一敬自然，风调雨顺赐福音，春去秋来收成好，窗前忙了晒秋姑。

Spring in Huangling

(Thoughts on the Most Beautiful Village in Wuyuan)

The path unseen in forest thick,

I ascend the peak amidst mountains,

Overlooking pear trees beneath.

Pear flowers floating on and on,

I read the book of spring at the end of mossy steps.

Note: Strolling on sloped roads and winding paths, I heard villagers talking in this Peach Blossom Spring. They said they loved the rustic lifestyle. They felt grateful that visitors enjoyed the breathtaking flowers, even though they are on the go all year round. They revered nature and prayed for good harvests. In spring they bustled about sowing seeds, for a spring drizzle was valuable as oil; in autumn women rush around drying grains in the sun.

十一　康定秋韵

Autumn in Kangding

冰川问

（游海螺沟有感）

林深避日芳草乱，万壑千岩竞秋装。
且问川冰春暖知，峰近几天不胜寒。

注：东海曾仙山，沧海说桑田，谁知波涛干涸日，留下海螺冰川；探海螺，访光阴，曾经有过无数，尽随秋风天边。飞索道，过穷林，迎面愁云片片，乘云已到山尽头，冰川何不见，只有身下乱石沙尘，好迷惘。忽有声，冰川在身下，何不见。正徘徊，仿佛有一玉女，满身泥土，蓬头垢面，曰：沧海桑田天地事，无意言，历尽洪荒篇篇。

Glaciers of Mount Gongga

Dense trees atop the mountain block the sunlight,

Requiring the tall grass beneath to grow by its own volition.

Valleys and ridges are dressed in autumn.

Only the crowns, which touch the clouds, lie bare.

If asked what season it is, they inevitably frown,

For they are capped with glaciers all year round.

Note: Wandering in Hailuogou Glacier Park, I saw traces of time everywhere I looked. Millions of years ago, Mount Gongga, on which Hailuogou Park lies, was an ocean trough. Over time, crustal plate movement has turned it into a huge mountain range located in west Sichuan Province. Glaciers cover its peaks all year round as a result of air currents and the freezing temperatures. Alas, everything has changed with the passage of time! In hopes of seeing the glaciers for myself, I followed a path upward, passing through dense woods and ascending grey clouds. I finally arrived at the top only to see nothing but jagged rocks and clouds of dust. I wondered where the glaciers were and suddenly heard a voice instructing me to look downwards. Lowering my head, I saw daylight being reflected off of a beautiful white glacier. I imagined it as a lovely young woman with fair skin and dark flowing hair. Silently, she showed me the masterpiece of nature and the vestiges of days past.

跑马溜溜山上

（游木格措有感）

金风寒露赏秋黄，置身蜀道知路难。

无怨峰险双飞翼，天近日短情丝长。

注：云山高，跑马溜，正是九月西风勤，信马雪莲山林秋。山路遥，过险道，登山云乱，横看群山低头，纵览天边彩霞，饮云岁月稠。昨夜风轻闻杜鹃，醒时睁眼霜吴姬。

Horseback in Mugecuo

The path is rough as I ride high up into the wooded mountains.

Trees have been yellowed by the autumn winds and are wet
with the morning dew.

Never have I been in such a bright and sunny mood.

I see two lovers riding up the mountain together.

They are worry free in their bliss despite the steep path and the
fleeting time.

Like wild geese floating freely with the wind.

Note: A western wind was blowing on that clear September morning. Atop my horse, I enjoyed the ride through the beautiful mountain scenery. I ascended the rough trail until I was surrounded by broken clouds. I took a break to take in the scenery. The mountains stood silently against the rosy light of dawn and the silver-lined clouds. I was reminded of stories of the past. Last night I was pulled from my sleep by a gentle breeze and the scent of azalea. I found that the mountain was capped with glaciers. It reminded me of a story in which the hair of a pretty young woman turned grey overnight. Alas, time always slips away without us even knowing!

木格措湖畔

（泛舟野人海）

青松枝、黄叶地，闲云秋水波依依。

问水临波天何处，随云 一片浪星际。

注：今到野人海，美丽听传说，无须辨真假，流光叹蹉跎；湖犹静，水依旧，片片碧波粼。女人似水，波深脉柔情，问今是何时，年复一年，听惯樵歌吟。

Rafting down the Savage Lake

Green pine branches and yellow leaves,

Wandering clouds and autumn waves,

Gazing into the water and seeing the reflection of the sky,

It felt like rafting on a cloud at such great heights.

Over time, I began to wonder where I was.

Note: I heard a beautiful legend about the Savage Lake. Whether it is real or not doesn't really matter because it has already become eternal over time. The lake is tranquil and still with the occasional blue sparkling waves. The gentle flow reminds me of a woman falling in love, as she gazes tenderly into her lover's eyes. Year after year, the songs of the lumberjacks can be heard on the bank of the lake, making people forget about the passage of time.

红石听泉

（观红石峡）

天碧透、云自悠，红石千载听泉流。

湍飞激石声声去，回眸群山又一秋。

注：跑马山高云天外，野人海畔雪莲开，径上九天听流泉，泉碧一线穿红台。红
台藏深谷，秋石斗奇彩。纵有世上多巧手，无奈天工妙安排。

Surging of the Redstone Gorge

In the mountains, the sky is azure and clear.

Clouds leisurely pass overhead.

The water has been surging along the Redstone Gorge for

thousands of years,

Striking the stones as it rushes past and away.

Time flies, and in an instant, another year has gone.

Note: I came to see Mount Pao Ma and the blooming ice lotuses on the Savage Lake.
On the mountaintop which touches the sky, I followed the sound of water and found
a thin stream of green water rushing through the deep vale. Even the most exquisite
workmanship pales in comparison to the glow of the many colored stones.

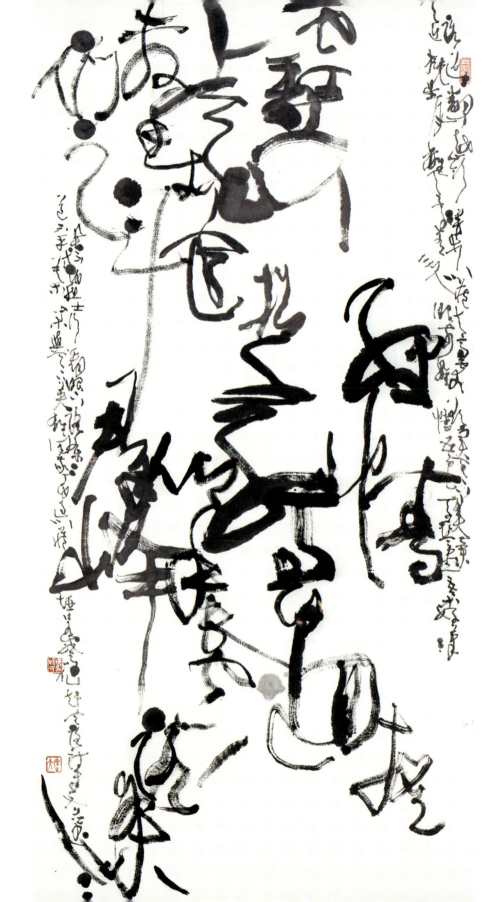

赶天路

（过垭口有感）

经幡摇、雪山招，千转百回上天道。

仰手长空搏牛斗，俯足群峰路条条。

注：路迢迢，翻山越岭，漫步川藏走高处。天近揽星月，欲赏天下美景，离天还有三尺，眼前锦幡五色，天蓝尽；吾等好汉，举杯酒胆壮行。看眼下路条条，道不平。莫等闲，与天下英雄同敬。

Travelling Along Tian Lu

We are greeted by prayer flags erected in the snowy mountain.

We gain altitude among the winding mountain paths.

With great ambition, I believe we can reach the peak.

We need only to glance behind for evidence of the arduous

journey.

Note: We climb the mountain road in order to enjoy an eagle eye view of the Tibetan Plateau. The sky is so close that the moon and stars seem to be within my reach. At this height we can truly enjoy the beautiful scenery. The blue sky provides a stunning backdrop to the colorful prayer flags. Before we leave, we have a toast in celebration and hopes that our friends can too conquer such a difficult and rewarding journey.

玉龙夕游

（新都桥观贡嘎雪山晚醉）

康定晚客新都她，闲马秋山叹夕霞。

搭手凉台西风起，横看玉龙醉贡嘎。

注：日暮晚风起，夜宿新都桥，群峰绿装渐卸，迎面落霞浸西。唯赏远处贡嘎，雪山素装含情。羞色托杯盘，问众山酒如何，时辰此值略醉意，常言道，酒至五分为好，尽兴已！

An Evening in Xinduqiao

I stayed a night in Xinduqiao and had a few sips of wine. In the distance,

Amid the glowing sunset, some horses were strolling among the autumn hills.

As I got dizzy after the drink, I rested my hands on the balcony rail.

The west wind rose, yet I felt not leaving.

In the drunk mood, I looked southwards, where

faraway, the Gongga Mountain lies in silence, as if

it was as tipsy as I was.

Note: Spending a night in Xinduqiao, I was having a drink in my room. The evening glow fell on the woods, and the green clothes of surrounding hills were gradually fading. The sun was falling into the west, and the Gongga Mountain standing under the evening sky, covered with white snow all around. A little tipsy at the time, I rose a cup of liquor and asked the mountains ahead how the wine was. Alas! My eyes were drunk with beauty, and my heart with joyfulness!

红叶金娘

（晨光霜叶新都桥）

清风晨曦静远岗，秋杨紫云野陌长。

昨夜寒霜红叶醒，硃霞锦处一姑娘。

注：甘藏空气薄，今夜难睡意。晨钟催，赶露稀。沿大道西行，树排排，山林密，一夜霜风艳娇色，绿黄红紫竞晨曦；远处姑娘早，点月眉，对镜云鬟看，红叶一片秋风里。

On the Autumn Leaves

(A Walk in Xinduqiao in the Morning Sunshine)

In the morning breeze, I see hills standing faraway.

The morning sunlight thrusts out, through purple clouds, onto

trees and wild grasses.

It was frosty last night, and now

the autumn leaves have all turned extremely red.

Dozens feet away from where I am standing, where the red

burns most brightly,

A beauty is doing her makeup carefully.

Note: The thin air in the Tibetan Plateau made it hard to sleep tight. So I woke up early in the morning and went out for a stroll when the dew had receded. Walking westward along the main path, I found trees there were densely planted. After a night of wind and frost, they had become even more beautiful, with leaves in green, yellow, red and purple competing for the warm sunshine in the morning. In the distance, amid the patches of gorgeous fall leaves, I saw a beauty doing her makeup carefully.

默牛霜草

（漫步新都桥天然牧场）

江南正是秋风爽，甘藏晨晚初寒霜。

霜草无意牦牛早，野高天旷无短长。

注：一夜秋风好景致，置身高原自不知，看落叶片片，野旷天低树；山前牦牛点点，直面寒风瑟瑟，林荫天边散牧场，数不清老牛新犊。问牛儿可好，尽低头，无所思，只顾眼下枯草，任天时。

Silent Yak Flock on a Frosted Grass Field

(A Promenade at the Pasture in Xinduqiao)

At this time of year, when it is still autumn in the South,

The Tibetan Plateau has already seen early frosts coming every night.

I see, early in the morning, that yaks were walking around,

Feeding themselves with frosted grass,

Under the canopy of the sky, on the boundless field,

Where time seems to have ceased to flow, in the vastness of space.

Note: With this beautiful scene brought by a night of autumn winds, I almost forget that I am now standing on the Tibetan Plateau. Leaves are falling from trees and in the boundless wild clouds hang atop the pasture. In front of the hills, there are a flock of yaks, full grown or cubs, strolling in the cold wind. They give me no response when I approach closer, only to lower their heads to eat withered grass, like nothing else would ever matter to their leisureliness.

十二　天府咏叹
The Land of Abundance:
Sichuan Province

柚园晚餐

野田轻径伴晚风，草篱翠色春意浓。
柚花一枝香无数，谈笑宾客散绿丛。

注：柚花扑鼻，香茗沁心，闲心尽情随香去，留下满腹疑云；此时正值春作忙，看柚田外，荒草片片，粮田狼藉，却无人问津。

Dinner in a Pomelo Orchard

The evening breeze blows over the pathways,
Spring turns the grass fence into bright green.
Pomelo flowers perfume the air,
Guests chat joyfully as they frolic about the orchard.

Note: I was relaxing in a pomelo orchard. Then I was seduced by the fragrance of pomelo flowers and the aroma of tea refreshed my mind. But when I laid my eyes upon the fields beyond the pomelo trees, I saw an expanse of unkempt grain fields left with no one to care for them. My good mood faded away and I began to worry …

水墨上理

（游雅安上理镇）

西岭远去雪霁色，东窗浅草寒溪开。
纵云天边飞石桥，林径声声马帮来。

注：蜀道难，上青天。自古马帮行滇川。鸟扶云，人栈道，商旅往返多艰辛。山林静，溪水清，美景多在险要处，商铺酒旗民风情。春风怒放勤学子，排排画架寻胜境，正本清源天地色，君子小人嘈杂音。

Picturesque Shangli Town

Seen from afar, snow continues to cap the mountains in the west.
However, in the east, streams are melting and the grass is growing.
A stone bridge stands strong on the breath-taking heights,
Out of the forest path chime the bells of a passing caravan.

Note: The road to Shu is arduous, even more so than climbing up to the heavens. Since ancient times, caravans have been transporting cargo through Yunnan and Sichuan. Birds soar high above the path as people traverse the cliffs by trestle road. Imagine how difficult it is for the merchants and travellers to come and go! But it is in the most dangerous places that you may find the most beautiful wonderful views. The mountain forests are tranquil and the streams are clear. Local pubs are decorated with self-designed flags to attract customers. Diligent students also come to discover and paint the beautiful spring sceneries with their brushes. If we wish to enjoy it, nature should be left to its own devices.

凤求凰

（临邛古码头有感）

春光无数巴地早，一曲清音百鸟嘈。

登桥吟风悠琴瑟，烟波生处凤还巢。

注：超越生命凤求凰，洗耳临邛鸟鹊巷，落霞尽头人潮动，众眼定神相如旁；文君本是富商女，雕楼深阁寡绣房。天地有尊卑，生命少年狂。道古今，爱情无须说理由，为爱生，为情死，谁懂吾心。

An Ancient Love Story

The sun shines brightly in Ba this morning,

The birds' ancient melody flows through the early spring air.

I walk on the bridge, listening to the beauty of nature.

Floating on the mist-covered water, a phoenix rises to return

back to its nest.

Note: In an alley in Linqiong (modern Qionglai, Sichuan), I heard beautiful music accompanied by birds singing. I remembered the over 2000-year-old love story about Sima Xiangru and Zhuo Wenjun. Sima Xiangru, a talented but poor man, played a song called *The Phoenix Woos His Mate* to Zhuo Wenjun, a wealthy iron manufacturer's widowed daughter. Having heard the song, Zhuo fell in love with Sima and ran away with him. Society may have its conventions, but younger generations always dare to ignore them. Love has never needed a reason or an explanation. We are born to love and die for love, and no one knows why.

十三　丽水烟霞

Glow in Lishui

舍利樟

（游古堰村）

蝉低鸣秋声，高节树雄魂。

风雷唤亘古，烈火锻真文。

注：古堰参神树，跪拜舍利樟。曾受雷电攻心，数遇烈火摧残，身已空，心不衰，皮坚枝繁百年。心无旁骛，往事逍遥去，九九苦难锻高节，载物华夏谱。

The Sarira Camphor Tree

(Thoughts on a Tour to Ancient Weir Village)

Cicadas sing an ode to the fall on the tree,

While the lofty spirit of the camphor rises up to the heaven.

For centuries it witnessed storms, thunder and flames,

Only with holiness can it survive all these disasters.

Note: The Sarira camphor tree is worshiped here. The tree survived one lightning strike and multiple fires. Hallow in trunk as it is, the tree never dies, standing straight for centuries, still exuberant and vibrant. Having been through countless hardships, the tree has stood the test of heaven with strong will and unswerving belief. Now that the past is left behind, this sacred tree will always be memorized in the river of history by generations.

古堰随想

（观通济堰）

古荫遮空郁文昌，青山避日丽水长。

纵堰横江济百渠，流响千载君何想。

注：千年堰堤，农桑通济，为官一方，民生心系。智慧造福爱百姓，子孙同德，江山绵远厚天地。看溪水依旧日东去，野田惆怅默无语。

Capriccio of the Ancient Weir Village

(A Visit to Tongji Weir)

In the shade of ancient trees lies Wenchang Pavilion,
Under the lush mountains flow many a beautiful stream and river.
The Tongji Weir, having nourished hundreds of ditches in fields,
Remains unchanged for thousands of years, echoing the past
and future.

Note: The Tongji Weir, as part of the water conservatory project, has been irrigating the local farmland for thousands of years since the 6th century. Officials of ancient times built the weir out of their concerns about the wellbeing of the local people. The weir facilitated their farming, protected them from floods and improved their lives. Harboring the same vision for a better life, generations of people have endeavored to develop this place. The farmland has been watching the rivers flowing to the east for thousands of years, knowing everything in silence.

双桥问

（游古堰过双桥）

烟花溪柳三月三，闲步堰廊赏春忙。

不识村淡桥水浅，万顷波涌藏三涵。

注：绿树村荫，文昌双桥过通济，桥平无意足下景，村姑引；陌路不知水深浅，更何知，桥下千尺三龙眠，望龙去，梦初醒，九天玄女叹先民。

Pondering over the Double Bridge

On the Spring Festival of local She people,

I take a walk along the causeway to enjoy the flowers and willows.

While outsiders see but the silent bridge and the gentle babbling brook,

Beneath rumbles the turbulent surge that will never idle away.

Note: Under the shade of trees lies the Double Bridge embodying prosperity, stretching over the Tongji Weir. Some village girls lead visitors across the bridge, paying no attention to the scenery around. The visitors have no idea how deep the water is, nor do they know that dragons are lying thousands of miles under. As they watch the dragons flying away, the dream ends, leaving only the goddess of the empyrean sighs over the ancient age.

画乡行

（游画乡古村）

春山淡抹隔江远，轻云临波羞野田。

极目沙渚横孤影，老街新肆待客船。

注：自古堰登舟，顺溪东走，溪鱼跳波，烟霞淡抹，峰切江口。见白鹭惊处，沙渚古樟漫游人，学子写生静墨眸。步岸离舟，沿街新肆老旗，各地政府打造文化待远客，春光虽好，何奈带不走乡愁。

A Tour to the Historical Village of Painting Countryside

The spring dresses the mountain with simple beauty,

The clouds drift over the river and the fields.

Some fishing boats lie around the distant sandbanks in solitary,

New shops open on ancient street, preparing for the day.

Note: I left the ancient weir by boat, and sailed along the stream to Huaxiang on the east. I saw fish swimming by the wave and the mountains opening the estuary for me. The thousand-year-old camphor tree was surrounded by tourists and sketching art students. Having gone ashore, I walked with leisure on the ancient street filled with newly-open shops in ancient style. Governments everywhere make efforts to rebuild traditional culture to attract tourists across the world these days. But no one can feel at home in these streets, even in such beautiful spring.

鳞田闲话

（丽水云和梯田有感）

东风夜雨翠山谷，镜面鳞田待花锄。
纵陌云岗笑春好，闲客安知农桑苦。

注：高山云田水空照，青陌紫萝赶春潮。春耕为时早，闲犊悠然尝新草。更喜天涯客，无惧峰险坡陡，问谁辛苦，听绿云倾诉。

On the Terraced Field

The east wind brought spring drizzle that turned the valley
green overnight,
And the glistering terraced fields await farmers' hoe.
The travellers are fascinated by the beauty of spring,
But they can never see the farmers' hard work and suffering.

Note: Mountains are looking down at the terraced fields, where the water shows the reflection of sky. All plants are hurrying to grow and blossom in this flourishing season of spring. It is still early for the spring ploughing, so the buffalo are idly feasting on the newly-grown grass. Travellers from everywhere climb up the steep mountains with no fear, listening to the clouds in the azure sky telling the stories of the industrious people.

尚杨居

（访丽水杨家堂）

村口古樟风雨地，泥堂庭落尚杨居。

迢云百折峰田少，耕读山门道贤愚。

注：苍山青，墙泥黄，春回杨家堂。杨家不姓杨，改姓氏，孝武耀山民。忠君报国匹夫责，山河固，庶子情，马头青瓦双双连理影。

A Tour to Yangjiatang Village in Lishui

The aged camphor tree stands at the gate,

Guarding the ancient residence with muddy walls.

Below the clouds are winding mountains instead of fields,

While farmers and scholars debate at the doors.

Note: In spring I visited Yangjiatang, a traditional village with green mountains and muddy walls. Curiously "Yang" is not the dwellers' family name. The villagers named it after the courageous and patriotic family of Yang, to inspire the younger generations to be loyal to the country. The walls and tiles are reminiscent of the brave young men in ancient times, who had been far away from their home and family fighting for their own country.

岫田春晓

（丽水岫田古村有感）

平步青云天，月冷东山田。

鸡鸣牧童早，桃李报村前。

注：岫田孤深山，百年话农桑，农桑无计风霜苦。崎道强童子，村陌榜眼遗风在，隔不断，通天路，云耕雾读说金屋。仁喜山，智乐水，有说新房好，也有爱旧屋，寡欲厚德修人性，乐无数。

A Spring Morning in Xiutian Village

The moon shines through the dark clouds,

With chilly light casted on the fields.

The herdsman's kid wake up early as the rooster,

Beginning his day with diligent morning reading.

Note: Life has been a struggle for the farmers in the remote and mountainous Xiutian Village for centuries. The roads are tough, but the kids here will not be stopped from going to school. The village is Confucius once said, the virtuous find pleasure in hills while the wise find pleasure in water, just as some favor new houses while some love the old ones. The endless happiness does not come with vanity and desire, but morality and merits.

十四　黔岭寨子

A Village Tour Along
Guizhou Ridge

老人与牛

（过银潭侗寨看斗牛房有感）

广宇空寒过流星，孤台侗戏唱古今。

牛郎七夕待会期，老汉无嗣牛同寝。

注：侗寨悠悠，古今特有，廊桥鼓楼，戏台伴牛，牛奉神灵，人老无酬。全寨共资，老汉五保，其职司牛，全为角斗。看不尽，中华南北多奇事，独此处牛人一房，吃住相守。

The Old Man and the Bull

Beneath the dark and empty night sky lit up by meteors,

Dong opera are telling tales old as time on a lonely stage.

In the tales Niulang waited longingly for the reunion at Qixi Festival,

While in reality an heirless old man lives with his bulls as if they were his sons.

Note: The time-honored Dong village is celebrated for covered bridges and drum towers. Bullpens are built near opera towers and bulls are honored as sacred. There is an old man in the village who has no income and children. Warm-hearted villagers donated money to him so he can raise bulls for bullfighting. It is said that he lives under the same roof with bulls, which I have never heard of.

水潺潺兮

（访银潭侗寨）

青山历尽黔东南，苗岭侗寨丽水旁。
古往山水忧伤多，任凭仁智道短长。

注：山道梁，苗家廊，水帐幔，清流之处侗寨安。安邦忘文字，侗戏唱四方。生旦丑末净，一台一牛房。问戏台，何时牛宿人床。

A Visit to the Picturesque Dong Village

There are no other mountains like those in east-south Guizhou
Province,
With Dong villages along Miaoling Valley nestling by its side
next to the scenic stream.
Such unspoiled place is nowhere to be found,
Unlike all those tarnished mountains and rivers.
Confucius once said, "The wise love water and the kind love
mountain,"
Let them argue, for I will love them all.

Note: The Miao and Dong peoples live here, where the tough mountains stretch and the clear water flows. The Dong culture is passed on through Dong opera rather than written texts. They tell stories of all people, of the man and the bull. Alas, perhaps we can ask those performers since when bulls share the same bed with people.

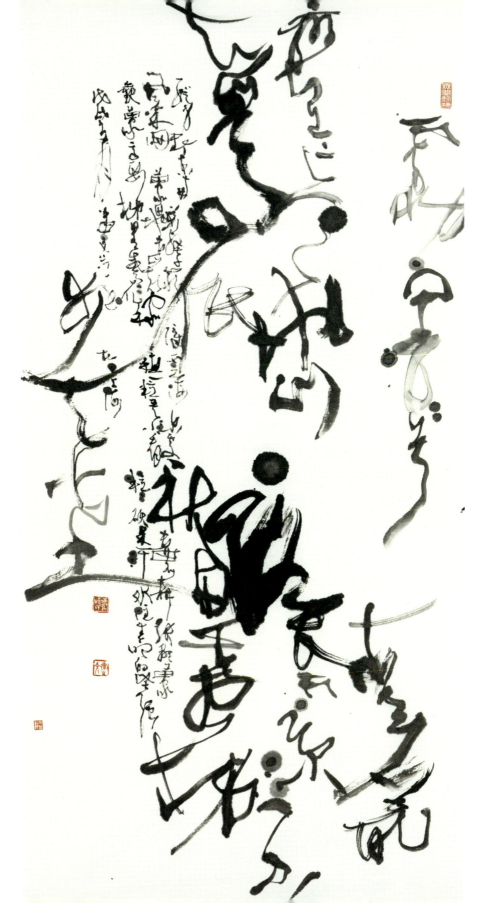

天道酬勤

（观苗家高要梯田）

雾漫漫兮青石乱，蛮荒之地山路长。

云深不知山高低，秋田随梯步天堂。

注：纵身黔东南，万壑千岩障，云海深处尽农耕，彰显苗家风采网。苗家田亩尽山巅，稼穗一粒莫小看。粒粒硕果汗水注，生命的坚强。

No Sweat, No Sweet

The dense fog shrouds scattered gravels,

On the long and winding trails.

Thick clouds capping the top of the mountains,

One can only see the rice terraces tower above leading to

heaven.

Note: In the mountainous east-south Guizhou Province, you can see expanses of farmland, on which the Miao people are toiling. Each ear of grain, as small as it is, comes from hard working.

乡愁风雨桥
（夜宿肇兴侗寨青定大酒店）

华灯初上钟鼓楼，巷深秋静溪水悠。
几度廊桥领风雨，一宿行人感乡愁。

注：初到肇兴，日落山隐。夜步侗寨品异乡，赏不尽霓虹商景。漫步风雨桥，曲水旧时景，灯观处处游人急，远处鼓楼暗静，几朝风雨几朝明，与谁同行。

Homesickness

The glamorous lights lit up the Bell and Drum towers,
While the stream flowed quietly by the alley.
Over the water the bridge witnessed countless rains and storms,
And all thc travellers with their homesickness in these nights
feeling lonely.

Note: I arrived at Zhaoxing at nightfall when mountains faded in the sunset. I wandered around wishing to savor the unfamiliar atmosphere of Dong village, where the neon signs lit up the stores by the streets. I came across a covered bridge overseeing the flowing river. The river will never stop slowing, regardless of the hustle and bustle next to it or the tranquility at the drum towers in the distance. I wonder how many rainy days the bridge witnessed, and how many travelers with my same thoughts.

天外音

（肇兴侗寨观侗家芦笙歌舞）

昨夜刚过风雨桥，不知何时来天庭。

上天只为听一曲，难比侗乐天外音。

注：侗寨犹静，光阴无形。不觉昨夜梦起时，又天明，好一曲芦笙涤尘雾，阴阳和五音；侗歌笙舞伴，隔山对鸳鸯，千年唱一曲，情深处，阿哥追身旁。

The Heavenly Reed-pipe Music

I walked past the covered bridge last night,

Only to find myself in heaven right now.

Such beautiful music deserves all the tough road here,

For there is nowhere else this can be heard.

Note: In the tranquil Dong Village, time ticks away slowly. I fell asleep, not knowing when. Woken up at dawn by the reed-pipe music, I heard the perfect harmony of yin and yang, of all sounds of nature, free from the vanity of the world. I saw girls and boys dancing to love songs across the hills. The boy couldn't help but fell for her, chasing her around singing all his heart and soul.

稻渔吟

（亮欢寨品酸汤鱼）

秋风寒露感乡音，稻渔篝火芦笙情。
且把人生畅怀酒，今夜无眠君莫停。

注： 今日客苗家，有酒当贵郎。灯火点点笙舞起，姑娘盛装。觞随歌勤，进门接杯饮，劝君要思量，莫言米酒淡，牛角绵绵醉意长。

Savoring Fish Soup

Cool autumn breeze and drops of dew sound like music from home,
While the bonfire and reed-pipe music are warm and joyful like the host.
Raise your glass to all the joyful moments in life.
Let's drink till the break of dawn as you will tonight.

Note: I was warmly treated by the Miao family with rice wine and local delicacies. Pretty Miao girls wearing traditional costumes dance by the bonfire, singing songs while serving me wine. Drink as much as you want when you step into the door, but think twice for the seemingly bland rice wine may leave you intoxicated.

十五　恩施骚客

A Journey in Enshi

蜉蝣地门

（游地缝有感）

长空淡漠太虚沉，云断青峰雾丘根。

蜉蝣临风鼓紫气，众生齐力开地门。

注：天薄何曾破大洞，地厚当年裂细缝。女娲补天无形迹，地缝尚存光阴穷。光阴一去不复返，区区蜉蝣朝夕共。朝夕共、天地蒙，上天为求生不老，入地不知欲何从。人不老、地不容，大地深处埋尸骨，无奈翁。问浩瀚星际，生命须勇气，前赴后继探极终。

Ephemera Gate

(At Yunlong River Geosuture)

The vibrant air deepening against boundless sky,

Green peaks break through mist to reach high.

Mayflies fluttering violet hazes with the wind,

All beings gathered to open the Ephemera gate.

Note: The thin sky never got a gaping hole, but the thick earth itself was once cracked and left a geosuture. The Goddess Nüwa mended the heaven without any traces left, but the geosuture was still there over time. Day and night, heaven and earth, mayflies gathered here. I knew they went up to heaven seeking immortality, but why did they enter the earth? Death befalls all men alike as bones were buried in the depths. I asked the vast universe and it responded that fresh ones should always entrust life to the courage, joining the existing ones to explore the ultimate proposition of life.

黄鹤桥魂

（游野三峡登临黄鹤桥）

晨风径禾平山浮，野云深岩藏惊图。

纵心桥天俯千秋，回眸望断云鹤路。

注：山重林迳，野田无垠，晨风晓行远眺，山丸浮轻云。云层层，道无穷，老夫试足黄鹤桥。左童鹤，右仙草，步履匆匆，误入红尘忘年少。白羽翔云端，黄鹤无去向，黄鹤自去无须问，请君驻足，静气平心。

Gone with Yellow Crane

(Ascending Yellow Crane Bridge at Wild Three Gorges)

Morning breeze passing through trails,

A startling scene hides in deep rocks and wild clouds.

On the Bridge high I bow to face a thousand autumns,

And glance back where cranes disappear.

Note: I fare forth at dawn in gentle morning breeze, overlooking endless path heading afar and light clouds floating around, jagged mountains and boundless wild fields. Rejuvenated, the old man sets feet on Yellow Crane Bridge, of left-hand leash, a young crane, on right hand wrist, the celestial herb. By mistake I sought mundane careers and forgot my youthful joy. Cleaving the air with white-plumed wings, the yellow crane leaves but who knows whither? No need to question but please stay, quietly and calmly enjoy this peace.

青岗白石听龙泉

（游石门河）

云岗天穷望愚公，蘽迷深谷降玉龙。
龙泉天底问白石，新水古地意何从。

注：苍穹青明，栈道云轻，曲直环形时隐，人随鸟行。忽闻足底深渊水响，闻声循径。白石嶙峋碧波，亲近问白石，何身白，身白计光阴。碎石守亿载，碧泉伴光影，看山外，几重天，时感山风凉，对波影，笑自白发吟。

Travelling Along Shimen River

Mountains soar into the cloud, bounding heaven narrow,

Waiting for its Yukong.

Luxuriant, deep, down the canyon descends a jade dragon of

water,

A dragon meandering between white rocks that I ask at the

bottom of heaven,

"Passing water or the ageless land — Which, tell me, shall my

heart follow?"

Note: Light clouds over a clear blue sky, I strolled on the plank road built on the face of cliffs. The road — now straight, now winding — vanished in my sight from time to time, but birds led my way. Suddenly there came deep down the canyon the sound of a river flowing. I tracked the sound and found the water rippling against pale white rocks. I got closer and whispered to them, "why are you so pale?" Then I knew the color was a proof of ancientness, a proof that these rocks have stood for hundreds of thousands of years, worn and broken by time. Noticing the sunlight blazing on the jade-pure surface of river, I turned to the sky between cliffs, and wondered how many worlds there were outside our own. In the cool breeze, I turned back to gaze at my reflection and, smiling, at the white-haired man who composed this poem.

上下求索
（清江画廊千瀑峡）

楚云一线楚天茫，清江青峰对两岸。
千丝纵恨叹绝壁，上下求索机布长。

注：天阴晴，楚水行，两岸青峰品波音，纵看楚天云雾色，江山如画，彩霞流星。云水深处，银泉往返，上下求索千年勤。一漱清漪多少事，挽起古今片片，问屈子，如今安好，碧波尽头屈子离骚吟。

Ascending and Descending in Search
(Thousand Waterfalls Gorge at Qingjiang Gallery)

A sliver of southern cloud floats in boundless southern sky,
Green cliffs of Qingjiang gradually unfold.
A thousand threads of water down the precipice in grief,
Ascending and descending in search, the cloth weaves long.

Note: Now cloudy, now clear, I travelled to the Yangtze roaring across green peaks, savoring its waves. The southern sky cloudy and foggy though, in the painting of the river and mountains, shooting stars shine in rosy afterglow. Amid clouds silver waterfalls plunging to the river, a thousand years, never stop ascending and descending to pursue the search. So many momentous events, past and present, disappeared in one glittering ripple. I ask, beyond emerald waves, how is Qu Yuan now? The chanting of *Li Sao* came from distant horizon.

十六　富春山居

Dwelling in the Fuchun Mountains

夜舟新安江

湖光初月泛晚舟，新风山民向牵牛。
此值广寒路几许，赋手横桨捧北斗。

注：建德新安江，古往多名人，两岸苍山增秀色，江水藏锦囊。江山代代，新波旧浪，丽水安居，人勤寿长。望江水，一路向东无尽时，人间天上。

Night Boating on Xin'an River

New moon shimmering on the lake, at night I boat.

A fresh breeze, in the mountain

Folk may turn to the Cowherd.

Wondering how long it would take

Travelling to the Guanghan Palace,

My hands off the paddle

Cupped around the Northern Dipper.

Note: Xin'an River of Jiande is known for being home to many nobles since ancient times, but the praise to its scenery never dims, particularly when mountains along the river grace its natural beauty. The river encircled, in my eyes, is a treasure flowing out from the embroidered purse of mountains, both of which have been through ages. New waves, old waves, they are blurred into this one graceful river that feeds people living along it, who work hard and live a long life. The endless river flows all the way east, turning lands it passes heaven on earth.

访古城严州

乌龙山下说风雨，三江口前辨涟漪。

临风古城望光阴，一波万载悠悠去。

注：又正六月，荷风酷意，闲来江南访古城，一路严州话题。步江堤，登城楼，诗画富春，古今六万秋；念地沉沉，天悠悠，时空太虚密不透，谁知光阴新旧。

On Yanzhou

Immersed in the beauty of Wulong Mountain,

I was wondering and counting the ripples of the river.

Winds howling on the old gate tower, I watch

The time flowing — waves of ten thousand years.

Note: Another June when the cool breeze brings the scent of lotus, I visited Yanzhou in Jiangnan at leisure. Talking about the ancient town all the way, we walked along the river and climbed the gate tower. Picturesque and poetic, though, Fuchun has been through sixty thousand autumns. How boundless and endless the heaven and earth are. Time, space, and universe are too hard to see through, so who knows the age of time?

老龙井

（龙井村品茶）

春下狮峰林泉新，五老村前道龙井。

一叶青茗天地色，沥尽人间甘苦情。

注：龙井泉老，狮峰茶新，不知泉老指何年，新茶年年采清明。老泉新茶贡皇家，为悦龙颜忙百姓。天道无常四时变，龙井村里道龙井。

Aged Longjing Tea

I visited the old spring in the ancient village of Longjing under the Lion Peak.

Longjing tea tastes best in the springtime.

As I sipped the tea, the truth of the universe seemed to unfold before my eyes.

It was as if I could taste the beauty of life.

Note: The spring near Longjing Village is centuries-old and the tea made under the Lion Peak is fresh. Nobody knows for certain how old the spring really is, however, the Longjing leaves turn green each year prior to the Qingming Festival. In the past, the common people brewed tea painstakingly every year for only the emperor to enjoy. Now, after centuries of drastic changes, it's my turn to taste Longjing tea.

荷田倩影

山禾溪柳忙低蝉，无心翠色芳荷田。

伶香一枝遥空碧，泥墙倩影清风前。

注：柳蝉声声，美丽乡村，匆匆山路尽翠色，十里长荷香如故。香消暑意，闲客尽兴，农夫辛苦，国泰民安勤为本，闻鸡起舞；数新房，寻旧屋，叹苍山，望长水，江南美景收不尽，泥墙水田寂寞。

A Shadow of Lotus in the Field

Stream rippling and cicadas singing on willows,

Lotus scent in the innocent green field,

A flower sways gently under the cloudless azure,

Leaving its shadow on a mud wall in a cool breeze.

Note: It's indeed a pretty cottage with cicadas singing on willows. All the way down the mountain road it was all green, and the same perfume of endless lotus flowers relieved the summer heat. Leisured visitors enjoyed themselves, but peasants worked hard in the field. That's our belief — diligence is essential for a country's prosperity and peace. I counted new houses while seeking the old ones. Lush mountains and lucid waters, impressed by Jiangnan view, I felt the loneliness of fields and the mud wall beside.